Spelunking Scripture:
Acts and the General Epistles of the New Testament
Exploring Important Passages of the Bible

BRUCE C. SALMON

© 2021
Published in the United States by Nurturing Faith, Macon, GA.
Nurturing Faith is a book imprint of Good Faith Media (goodfaithmedia.org).
Library of Congress Cataloging-in-Publication Data is available.

ISBN: 978-1-63528-159-0

All rights reserved. Printed in the United States of America.

All scripture citations are from the New Revised International Version (NRSV) unless otherwise indicated.

Cover: A stained glass window in St. Columb's Cathedral in Northern Ireland, depicting stories from the Book of Acts. From left to right: the ordination of St. Stephen the first Christian martyr, a quote from St. Peter when he heals a lame man, and St. Peter being freed from prison by an angel as the guard sleeps.

Contents

Introduction v

Chapter 1: You Will Receive Power 1
The Absence of Christ (Acts 1:6-14) 1
Now What? (Acts 1:1-14) 5
You Will Receive Power (Acts 1:1-9) 8

Chapter 2: The Holy Spirit 13
The Gift of the Holy Spirit (Acts 2:1-4, 37-39) 13
Filled with the Spirit (Acts 2:1-4) 17
One in the Spirit (Acts 2:1-21) 19

Chapter 3: The Seven 23
Chosen to Serve (Acts 6:1-7) 23
Waiting on Tables (Acts 6:1-7) 26
At Your Service (Acts 6:1-7) 28

Chapter 4: Run The Race 31
All the Way Home (Heb. 12:1-2, 12-13) 32
Rediscovering Our Spiritual Focus (Heb. 12:1-2) 35
A Cloud of Witnesses (Heb. 12:1-2)) 38

Chapter 5: Let Mutual Love Continue 41
Sacrifices Pleasing to God (Heb. 13:1-5, 16) 41
Hospitality to Strangers (Heb. 13:1-2, 16) 43
The Grass Is Always Greener (Heb. 13:1-5) 45

Chapter 6: Faith and Deeds 49
Living Faith (Jas. 2:8-17) 49
If Jesus Is Lord (Jas. 2:1-17) 52
Faith Works (Jas. 2:14-17) 54

Chapter 7: Pray for Each Other 59
The Power of Prayer (Jas. 5:13-16) 59
Pray for One Another (Jas. 5:13-16) 62
The Power of Prayer (Jas. 5:13-16) 64

Chapter 8: New Birth Into a Living Hope 69
    The Outcome of Your Faith (1 Pet. 1:3-9) 69
    Footsteps in the Concrete (1 Pet. 1:1-9) 72
    Black Swans and the Love of God (1 Pet. 1:3-9) 74

Chapter 9: The Hope That is in You 77
    The Hope That is in You, Part 1 (1 Pet. 3:8-17) 77
    The Hope That is in You, Part 2 (1 Pet. 3:13-18) 81
    The Hope That is in You, Part 3 (1 Pet. 3:13-18) 83

Chapter 10: Love One Another 87
    Love in Action (1 John 4:7-8) 87
    Who Cares? (1 John 4:7-21) 90
    Three Levels of Love (1 John 4:7-11) 93

About the Author 97

Introduction

There is no shortage of books about the Bible. When I was in seminary, students were referred to biblical commentaries, scholarly volumes that provide background and contextual information, and verse-by-verse commentary on each book of the Bible. Commentaries were available in multi-volume sets covering the entire Bible, and as individual volumes on specific books of the Bible, usually written by academicians who had done extensive research. My prized commentary sets back then were *The Interpreter's Bible* (1952), edited by George Buttrick, and *The Broadman Bible Commentary* (1969), with several volumes written by some of my seminary professors. I also valued a commentary set on the New Testament, *The Daily Study Bible Series* (1975), by William Barclay.

More recent commentary series that I have used include *The New Interpreter's Bible* (1994), *Zondervan Illustrated Bible Backgrounds Commentary* (2002 & 2009), *Interpretation: A Bible Commentary for Teaching and Preaching* (2009), and the *Smyth & Helwys Commentary* series (2018). Apart from commentary sets, there are many excellent individual commentaries on individual books of the Bible. Some commentaries are written for a more popular audience, while others are geared toward preachers, teachers, and other readers with some theological education. The aim of most commentaries is to explain what the Bible says. Their focus is on the "what" question of biblical interpretation.

This series, *Spelunking Scripture*, moves beyond the "what" question to the "so what" question. Of course, it is important to know "what" the Bible says. But the "so what" question moves biblical interpretation to another level. It asks, "So what does this scripture passage say to me?" It moves from the theoretical to the practical, from biblical literacy to life application. That essentially is the purpose of most sermons. The preacher moves from explaining what the text says, to explaining what the text says to us.

I gave my first sermon the summer after my freshman year in college. In almost 50 years of preaching, my goal has been to move from the biblical text to our present-day situation. I seek to explain the meaning of the text for the original readers, and then to suggest what the text might mean for us today. Thus, I seek to move from "what" does the text say, to "so what" does it have to do with us? "Spelunking scripture" explores important passages of the Bible for the purpose of discovering their relevance to modern-day life. Just as spelunking involves a personal exploration of underground passages of caves, so spelunking scripture involves a personal exploration of important passages of the Bible.

I served as pastor of Village Baptist Church in Bowie, Maryland (outside Washington, D.C.) for 33 years, from the beginning of 1985 until early 2018. After I retired, my wife Linda and I began attending the First Baptist Church of the City of Washington, D.C. At first, we only attended worship, sitting most Sundays with our good friend Dr. James Langley, retired executive director of the D.C. Baptist Convention. After Dr. Langley died in June of 2018, we moved our membership to First Baptist Church, in tribute to him, and to make a deeper connection with our new church family.

As part of that deeper connection, we joined an adult Sunday School class called Crossroads. Instead of one person teaching the class, various class members alternated as facilitators, leading discussions on a series of books that we read together. We read and discussed such thought-provoking books as *The Cross and the Lynching Tree* by James Cone, and *Falling Upward* by Richard Rohr. But the study books that were most meaningful for me were those based on passages of scripture.

I especially appreciated two mini commentaries, *Reading John for Dear Life: A Spiritual Walk with the Fourth Gospel* by Jaime Clark-Soles, and *Sessions with Genesis* by Tony Cartledge. Not surprisingly, during my many years as a pastor, I had studied and taught the Gospel of John and the book of Genesis many times. In fact, I had preached sermons on Genesis 67 times, and I had preached sermons on John 181 times. But Jaime Clark-Soles and Tony Cartledge did more than explain what those books/passages might have meant to the original readers. These writers offered suggestions as to what those passages might have to say to our time. They were "spelunking scripture," although they did not call it that! Clark-Soles called her approach "a spiritual walk with the fourth Gospel." Cartledge also sought to identify spiritual lessons in his short commentary. Both Jaime Clark-Soles, professor of New Testament at Perkins School of Theology at Southern Methodist University and a frequent preacher in churches, and Tony Cartledge, professor of Old Testament at Campbell University Divinity School and a former pastor, are biblical scholars who recognize the importance of moving beyond an academic exegesis of scripture to a practical application.

Another mini commentary that our Crossroads class read and discussed was *The Forgotten Books of the Bible* by Robert Williamson Jr., who teaches at Hendrix College in Arkansas and is the founding pastor of Mercy Community Church in Little Rock. Unlike the commentaries by Clark-Soles and Cartledge, Williamson covered biblical books that I was less familiar with. His book explores "the Five Scrolls" of the Old Testament, namely, Ruth, Esther, Ecclesiastes, Song of Songs, and Lamentations. Although I knew what the books were about, I had rarely preached on them. In 33 years, I preached one Sunday morning sermon on Ruth, two on Esther, six on Ecclesiastes, one on Song of Songs, and two on Lamentations. I preached so few sermons based on passages from those books because I considered them to be less important than many other books of the Bible. Yet, even less-important books of scripture can convey important messages.

My study on Acts and the Epistles is part of the series, *Spelunking Scripture*. Recently published volumes focus on the Christmas story and the letters of Paul in the New Testament. Forthcoming volumes will explore the Easter story, important passages from the Gospels, and significant portions of the Old Testament. This present volume explores the Acts of the Apostles and the general epistles of the New Testament. Admittedly, identifying which passages of scripture are the most important is more art than science. One criterion might be selecting those that are quoted or referenced in other parts of the Bible. Another criterion might be choosing sections that reflect major themes of the Bible. The primary criterion is Christ. For Christians, Jesus is the criterion by which we interpret all of scripture.

After I retired, I wrote a book, *Preaching for the Long Haul: A Case Study on Long-Term Pastoral Ministry*. During the writing of the book, I catalogued the text and title of every original Sunday morning sermon I had preached at Village Baptist Church over the course of 33 years. Although the first 15 years of sermon manuscripts were burned up in my office by the fire that destroyed the church building in January of 2000, I had brought home the sermon notes during those years. Thus, I was able to reconstruct a list of every sermon title and scripture text for almost 1,500 sermons preached over 33 years. In reviewing those sermon titles and texts, I discovered that I had preached on some texts many times:

- Luke 2 at least 29 times
- the Sermon on the Mount in Matthew 5 at least 24 times
- the story of the Wise Men in Matthew 2 at least 20 times
- Pentecost in Acts 2 at least 18 times

How is it possible to preach on the same scripture passage again and again and have something new to say? It is a matter of spelunking scripture. It is a matter of moving beyond the "what" question to the "so what" question of the scripture text.

My method in spelunking scripture is to identify and explore important passages with a brief introduction and three studies/sermons on each text. At the end of each chapter, some questions for discussion/reflection prompt the reader to make your own move from "what" to "so what." Thanks for joining me on another spelunking expedition through some of the most important passages of the Bible.

CHAPTER 1

YOU WILL RECEIVE POWER
(Acts 1:6-9)

> *"It is not for you to know the times or dates the Father has set by his own authority. But you will receive power when the Holy Spirit comes on you; and you will be my witnesses in Jerusalem, and in all Judea and Samaria, and to the ends of the earth." After he said this, he was taken up before their very eyes, and a cloud hid him from their sight.*
>
> (Acts 1:7b-9 NIV)

We call it the Ascension. The Risen Jesus was taken up out of the disciples' sight. After the resurrection, he had appeared to them over a period of 40 days and had spoken to them about the kingdom of God. But he would not remain with them in a visible form forever. The book of Acts functions as the second volume of the Gospel of Luke. It continues where the gospel left off, with Jesus commissioning his disciples to proclaim his name to all the nations.

The Ascension is described briefly in Luke 24:51, and again in Acts 1:9. While Luke tells the story of Jesus in the flesh, Acts tells the story of Jesus continuing to be with the disciples through the Holy Spirit. The book is traditionally called "The Acts of the Apostles," but it also could be called "The Acts of the Holy Spirit." Luke's purpose in writing Acts was to show that the story of Jesus he began telling in his gospel was not over, not by a long shot. The story continued as the followers of Jesus, empowered by the Holy Spirit, began to take the gospel, the good news, to the ends of the earth.

THE ABSENCE OF CHRIST
(Acts 1:6-14)

I think I understand some of what the disciples felt when Jesus ascended into heaven. In August of 1988, we took our 15-year-old daughter Amy to National Airport near Washington, D.C. Her 44-pound bag had been carefully packed. She had her ticket, passport, and travelers checks in hand. We had been preparing ourselves for that day for a long time. Still, when Amy finally got on the airplane to take off for her year as an exchange student in France, all of us were upset.

Amy was crying, Linda was crying, and our son Marc and I felt like crying. We knew where she was going. We knew one day she would be coming back. Still, when Amy disappeared out of our sight, it was hard to take. There was a lump in our throats and an emptiness in our hearts. It was hard to get used to the fact that she would not be around anymore, at least not for a long time.

As we were driving out of the airport parking lot, none of us wanted to go home. It would seem too lonely there with just the three of us. So, we did what most Americans do when they are depressed: we went shopping. It wasn't all that exciting. We drove from National Airport to Springfield Plaza in Virginia to the new Baptist Book Store that had recently opened. That took our minds off Amy for a while. But eventually, we did return home, and the house did seem empty.

It took a long time for us to get used to that empty place at our kitchen table. Remember, this was before cell phones, before the Internet, before easy communications around the world. We did make a long-distance international phone call to Amy in France on her birthday in December, but other than that, our only means of communication was through letters in the mail. Amy was gone from us, and we felt her absence every day.

I think I know how the disciples felt. They knew the day was coming when Jesus would no longer be with them. They knew where he was going, and they knew that eventually he would be coming back. Still, when Jesus disappeared out of their sight, it was hard to take. It left the disciples with a lump in their throats and an emptiness in their hearts. It would seem awfully lonely without him. But instead of going shopping as we did, they went back to Jerusalem, back to the upper room, back to the place where they had shared that last supper with Jesus on the night before he died. There in the upper room they gathered with the women followers, and Mary, his mother, and his brothers. And together they devoted themselves to prayer, clinging to the promise that somehow Jesus would be with them.

I realize not everyone has had the same experience we did of putting our teenage daughter on an airplane to send her off for a year in France. But most people have had their own experiences of loneliness and wistful absence. Some people have known even greater sorrow. Some know what it is like to come home from the cemetery after having laid a loved one to rest. Some know what it is like to sit in a doctor's examination room and hear the lab report that reads "malignant." Some know what it is like to have a close friend move away. Some know what it is like to leave the courthouse after the judge has declared the divorce final. Some know what it is like to receive that termination notice with the dreaded news that they no longer have a job. Some know what it is like to have a child leave home for college or the military or to get married.

Most of us have gone through some loneliness experience when it seems as if even God isn't around anymore. We talk so much about the presence of Christ, we might give the impression that the experience of God's nearness is a constant thing. But for many of us, it is not: there are times when Christ does not seem close at hand. We wonder exactly where Christ is in all of this. It's not that we have lost our faith or that we are without hope. It's just that in our world, and in the up-and-down experiences of our daily lives, the presence of Christ is sometimes fleeting. Sometimes our awareness of Christ's presence grows faint and dim.

It's not our fault. It's not God's fault. That's just the way life is. Jesus did not remain visible to the disciples forever. He vanished out of their sight. The question is: What do we do now? What do we do in those in-between times when God seems to disappear, and the reality of a hard situation smacks us square in the face? What do we do when a loved one dies, or the diagnosis is cancer, or the job gets terminated, or the friend moves away, or the child leaves home, or the marriage breaks up, or any one of a thousand other possibilities comes along? What do we do when God seems distant or nowhere to be found? We talk so much in church about the presence of Christ, but what do we do when Christ is absent? Here is what we do:

First, we realize we are not the only ones who have felt that way. The absence of God is not a strange or unusual phenomenon. In fact, for most people, God seems distant at some point in their lives. The Bible is filled with people who experienced God's absence. King David was a man as close to God as any human, and yet there were times when he wondered where God was in his life. Read some of his psalms:

> Why are you so far away, O Lord?
> Why do you hide yourself when we are in trouble?
> (Ps. 10:1, GNT)

> How much longer will you forget me, Lord?
> How much longer will you hide yourself from me?
> How long must I endure trouble?
> How long will sorrow fill my heart night and day?
> (Ps. 13:1-2b, GNT)

> I have cried desperately for help, but still it does not come.
> During the day I call to you, my God, but you do not answer.
> I call at night, but get no rest.
> (Ps. 22:1b-2, GNT)

These psalms were written by the same David who could also write great psalms of praise: "The Lord is my shepherd, I shall not want" (Ps. 23:1). "The Lord is my light and my salvation; whom shall I fear" (Ps. 27:1). The point is that David's experience of God was not consistent. Even though he was a great person of faith, David had his high points and his low points. So did most of the great people of faith in the Bible. The prophet Elijah could stand up for God with courage on Mount Carmel, and then go into a deep depression as he hid in a cave on Mount Horeb, wondering where God was. Isaiah, Jeremiah, and Ezekiel all had their moments when God seemed very near, and then moments when God seemed far off. Even Jesus cried from the cross, "My God, my God, why have you forsaken me?" For some reason, God does not always seem near.

More than 300 years ago there was a young man growing up in France named Nicholas Herman. At the age of 18 he had a personal religious experience and decided to become a monk. He was not an educated man. He was not a particularly talented man. But over the years he developed a reputation as a man who was close to God. They called him Brother Lawrence, and he served the other monks by working in the monastery kitchen. He was a man of humility and simplicity. Brother Lawrence said he could worship God as easily in the kitchen as he could in the cathedral. He felt as close to God scrubbing pots and pans as he did on his knees in church. Brother Lawrence had a simple prayer:

> Lord of all pots and pans and things…
> Make me a saint of getting meals
> And washing up the plates!

We know about Brother Lawrence because of the letters he wrote, some of which have been preserved. The letters were compiled into a small book called *The Practice of the Presence of God*, which has become a devotional classic read by countless people. The subtitle of the book is: "The simple wisdom of a man who felt the constant companionship of God." And yet, even for Brother Lawrence, that companionship with God was not always constant. He wrote in one of his letters: "God has many ways of drawing us to Himself. He sometimes hides Himself from us." Imagine that! Even a great Christian mystic, a man of prayer like Brother Lawrence, knew times when God was hidden. Yet, he went on to say, when God is hidden from us, "faith alone ought to be our support, and the foundation of our confidence." This is a lesson we can learn from the disciples.

Just as Christ seemed absent from the disciples and Brother Lawrence, Christ may be absent at some point in our lives—invisible, nowhere to be seen. We can gaze up into heaven until we get a crick in our necks, but sometimes all we can see are the clouds. In times like these, there is no need to panic, no need to despair, no need to fear. Moments of the hiddenness of God come to most people. We can learn from the disciples that in times when Christ is absent, faith will see us through.

Religious feelings come and go. Emotions fluctuate. But faith is not an emotion. Faith is a conviction, a confidence, the sure foundation we can stand upon when the ebb and flow of the tides of life wash over us. Faith will not fail us in time of need. But some doubters might say, "My faith is not strong enough." That's what the church is for. Notice that the disciples did not scatter after Jesus ascended into heaven. They didn't wander off or each return to his own home. They stayed together. They went back to the upper room where they had been with Jesus, and they joined with other believers in prayer.

When God seems absent, when our faith seems weakened, we need to go back to the place where we have been with Jesus. Go back to church, go back to the fellowship of believers, go back to the Bible, go back to worship, go back to prayer. Sometimes God can use his hiddenness to make us stronger. In times when God seems absent, go back to the places where God may be found. We fall back on our faith, on the church, on our Christian friends.

Counselors use a term called "ego borrowing." The idea is that sometimes persons in counseling have such a poor self-image, such low self-confidence, that they need to borrow some ego strength from the counselor. The same can work with faith. Sometimes we need to borrow faith from other Christians. When our own faith is weak, we need to let the faith of others lift us up and carry us along.

There is a third lesson in all of this: God never really leaves us. Oh, sometimes we may not sense his presence. Sometimes God is hidden from us. Sometimes the clouds block our view. Sometimes the problems of life crowd in around us so that we cannot see God. But God is present nevertheless. The last thing Jesus said before he vanished from the disciples' sight was to assure them of his presence through the Holy Spirit. Jesus was still with them, just in a different way. No longer was he among them physically; now he was within them in spirit.

Rollo May, in his book, *Man's Search for Himself*, writes that the task of life for every person is to "find centers of strength within ourselves." We can do that. When the loneliness and sadness of life come upon us, we can find centers of strength within ourselves. That is because the center of strength within the heart of every believer is the Spirit of the Risen Christ.

Our daughter Amy spent almost a year away from us in France. But the following July she came back home, and it was a time of great celebration. Yet, in our hearts, she never really left us. So it is with the Risen Christ. He's coming back. One day he will return in all his glory. One day all the earth will be gathered up in a great festival of celebration. One day we will see him face to face. But in our hearts, he never really left. His Spirit is the quiet center of strength within ourselves. It just may be that when Christ seems absent, he is most near.

NOW WHAT?
(Acts 1:1-14)

Life is full of "now what?" moments. Beginnings, endings, transitions, changes…life never stands still. A baby is born…now what? A student graduates…now what? A couple gets married…now what? A job position is eliminated…now what? A loved one dies…now what? A person accepts Christ and is baptized…now what? Life is filled with "now what?" moments. It is what we do with those "now what?" moments that determines what our lives will be.

Our scripture was a "now what?" moment for the followers of Jesus. It was after Jesus had died on the cross and been resurrected from the grave. The Risen Christ had appeared among the disciples for 40 days. Now, he was preparing to leave them. They would no longer be able to see him with their eyes or hear him with their ears or touch him with their hands. Soon the Risen Jesus would be gone from their presence, and they would have to figure out how to get along without him. It would have been natural for the followers of Jesus to feel lost and afraid and terribly lonely at the thought of Jesus leaving them. But Jesus told them to wait for the promise of the Father. He told them that John the Baptist had baptized with water, but soon they would be baptized with the Holy Spirit. Not only that, but they also would receive power when the Holy Spirit came upon them, and they would be his witnesses in Jerusalem and Judea and Samaria and to the ends of the earth.

Then, as they were watching, Jesus was lifted up and a cloud took him out of their sight. As they were staring up into the sky, two figures appeared and asked them, "Why do you stand looking up to heaven?" In other words, the angels asked them, "now what?"

Now that Jesus was gone, what were they going to do next? It was, in fact, a challenge to get on with their lives. It was a summons to make the transition from being led by Jesus to being led by the Holy Spirit. Jesus would no longer be there to guide them, but the Holy Spirit would fill them with power. It was one of those crucial "now what?" moments in life. Jesus was gone from their sight—now what?

We call this event the Ascension. The Risen Jesus ascended into heaven and no longer appeared to his followers in a physical, visible, bodily way. After being with them for some three years, now he was gone. And they had to figure out what to do next when he was no longer there to lead them. Soon they would receive the Holy Spirit. That would happen just a few days later at Pentecost. But Ascension Day was one of those "now what?" moments.

After Jesus disappeared from his followers, and after the angels told them to stop looking up into heaven, they went back to Jerusalem to try to figure out what to do. They gathered in an upstairs room, perhaps the same upper room where Jesus had shared the Last Supper with them just six weeks earlier. There, the 11 remaining disciples gathered with the women followers of Jesus, including his mother Mary and his brothers. Together they devoted themselves to prayer in order to answer that "now what?" question that the ascension of Jesus presented to them.

Baptism is one of the most important moments in any Christian's life. It's a visible expression of faith, identifying with Jesus in his death, burial, and resurrection. Baptism signifies forgiveness from sin and new life in Christ. It's a high and holy moment, a spiritual mountaintop experience. In my Baptist tradition, a person who professes faith in Christ is baptized not only with water, but also with the Holy Spirit. That's one reason why Baptists practice believer's baptism (and not infant baptism). Being baptized as believers means we can remember it for the rest of our lives. I don't remember anything that happened to me when I was a baby, but I remember my baptism because it was my decision to profess faith in Jesus and it was the beginning of my new life in Christ.

As with other significant events, baptism is one of those "now what?" moments. But it's only the beginning of our Christian journey, not the end. Every person, upon being baptized, must ask himself or herself, "now what?" Since I have accepted Christ into my heart, been baptized, and accepted into the fellowship of the church, now what?

Adoniram Judson was born in Malden, Massachusetts in 1788. His father was a Congregational minister, so he was baptized as an infant. That meant he was not aware of what was going on, since he was not old enough to decide for himself to follow Christ. Young Adoniram was a brilliant student. He entered the College of Rhode Island and Providence Plantations (now Brown University) at the age of 16 and graduated at 19. While studying at the college, he met a fellow student who challenged his childhood faith. This friend was a deist and a religious skeptic. He introduced Adoniram to the writings of the French philosophers, and soon he abandoned the religious instruction of his parents and became a skeptic too.

Then in 1808, at the age of 20, Adoniram Judson had an experience that would change his life. While sleeping in a room at an inn, Adoniram heard a man in another room become violently ill during the night. The next morning Judson asked about the other guests' health. He was told that the man had died. That was shocking enough, but then Judson learned that the dead man was his friend, the one who had led him away from the Christian faith. This terrible turn of events was a "now what?" moment for Adoniram Judson. It led him to a time of profound soul-searching. Eventually it led him to return to the faith of his youth.

After his friend died, Judson made a "solemn dedication of himself to God." Two years later, while a student at Andover Theological Seminary, Adoniram Judson dedicated himself to becoming a Christian missionary, to take the gospel to Asia. Judson and a few of his classmates presented themselves before the Congregational Church's General Association to appeal for their support. Impressed by the young men's respectful demeanor and religious fervor, the elders appointed Judson and the others as missionaries to the East.

On February 5, 1812, Adoniram Judson married his fiancée Ann. The next day he was ordained as a minister. Two weeks later Adoniram and Ann Judson set sail for India. Traveling with them were another newly appointed missionary couple and a single missionary named Luther Rice. During their four-month voyage to India, Judson and the others had plenty of time on their hands. They used that time to study the Scriptures, especially as the Bible related to the theology of baptism.

To their surprise, the Judsons and Luther Rice became convinced that baptism was for believers, not infants. They became further convinced that they should be baptized on the basis of their faith, despite having been baptized as babies. The Judsons and Luther Rice also concluded that they could not in good conscience remain Congregationalists and be supported as missionaries by the Congregational church. In fact, they decided to resign from the Congregational church and become Baptists.

Upon reaching India, Adoniram and Ann Judson, along with Luther Rice, sought out the British Baptist missionary William Carey and his associate William Ward. The Judsons and Rice were then baptized by immersion in Calcutta on the basis of their faith in Jesus. It was another "now what?" moment. Initially they intended to work alongside William Carey in his efforts to evangelize the Hindus in India. But the War of 1812 had begun back home, and Americans were not welcome in British-controlled India. Now what?

Adoniram and Ann Judson set sail for Burma, while Luther Rice returned to the United States to raise money for their support. Back in the U.S. in 1814, Luther Rice convened the first national meeting of Baptists, which formed the American Baptist Missionary Union. This was the beginning of the Baptist denomination, with churches coming together to support missionaries. Luther Rice spent a lot of time in Washington, D.C., and in 1821 founded Columbian College. That institution is now George Washington University, and the main administration building there is named Luther Rice Hall.

Back in Burma, Adoniram and Ann Judson spent years learning the Burmese language. Adoniram was a linguistic scholar, already fluent in Latin, Greek, and Hebrew, but he and his wife found a tutor and spent 12 hours a day learning Burmese. During their first few years in Burma, they were almost entirely isolated from any contact with

Europeans or other Americans. It was five years before they dared to hold a public gospel meeting. The first Burmese believer was baptized in 1819, and by 1823 there were 18 baptized believers in the Burmese church. So, it took the Judsons 10 years to win 18 converts. But during that time Adoniram developed a grammar of the Burmese language that is still available today, and he began to translate the Bible into Burmese.

When Adoniram and Ann Judson went to Burma, his goal was to translate the Bible and found a church. By the time Adoniram Judson died, he left behind the complete Bible in Burmese and more than 100 churches and 8,000 believers. Today, Burma, or Myanmar, has almost a million Baptist believers. And here in the United States there are at least 36 Baptist churches named after Adoniram Judson, in addition to Judson University in Illinois. (Judson College in Alabama, a private women's college founded in 1838 and named after his wife Ann, closed in 2021.)

There are many "now what?" moments in life. The Ascension was one of them for the early followers of Jesus. Baptism is one of those "now what?" moments for every believer. The first followers of Jesus answered their "now what?" moment by staying together in fellowship and by joining together in prayer.

That's a good model for all Christians: Stay together in fellowship and join together in prayer. Wait for the power of the Holy Spirit; then be witnesses in Jerusalem and Judea and Samaria and to the ends of the earth. We may not be able to cross the ocean and go to Burma as Ann and Adoniram Judson did, but we can be witnesses for Jesus in our own Jerusalem and Judea and Samaria. And we can support those who do go to the ends of the earth. We can be like Luther Rice and support our missionaries and do our part here at home. Even if you were baptized a long time ago, today can be a "now what?" moment for you. Or, if you have never been baptized on the profession of your faith in Jesus, today can be a "now what?" moment for you.

Life is filled with "now what?" moments. May we, filled with the Spirit, do something for Christ with our lives too.

YOU WILL RECEIVE POWER
(Acts 1:1-9)

It was October 27, 2012, the day before Superstorm Sandy would surge up the East Coast and slam onto Long Island. Richard and Samantha Specht were busy preparing their home for the approaching storm. Rich, an 8th grade science teacher, and Sam, a high school German teacher, were the parents of three children, daughters Abigail and Lorelei, ages 8 and 6, and son Rees, age 22 months. Samantha took the two girls and went to the store to stock up on supplies. Rich remained home with Rees and his best friend from childhood, Rees' godfather.

When Rich went to take some lawn furniture to the garage, he asked his friend to keep an eye on Rees. Later in the house Rich asked his friend where Rees was. His friend said, "I thought he was with you." The two men began to frantically search for the not-quite 2-year-old. Eventually they found him, lying face down in a backyard pond. Rich began to perform CPR while his friend called 911. Rees was rushed to the hospital, but it was too late. The boy had drowned.

The next day, as the hurricane pounded Long Island, the family began to make funeral arrangements. The power went out, and they spent the next 11 days without electricity. Since many cell towers were down, they had to drive to the post office to get a signal strong enough to make phone calls. As word of the tragedy spread, friends and neighbors did whatever they could to help. Even people they did not know wanted to do something. A local landscaper heard what had happened and offered to fill in the backyard pond, at no charge. Everyone worked to recover from the devastation of the storm, but the Spechts had to recover from the even greater devastation of the loss of their son. Even after electricity was restored, the Spechts would need another kind of power to carry on.

Rich and Sam were bereft, as any parents would be, but they knew they could not give in to grief. They had two daughters who needed them more than ever. So, they decided that the best thing they could do to remember their son was to set up a foundation in his honor. They named the foundation, ReesSpecht Life. They were so grateful for the many kindnesses they had received following Rees' death. They could not pay everyone back, but they could use the foundation to encourage others to perform acts of kindness in memory of their little boy. They even had cards printed up with Rees' picture on them that people could give out whenever they did something to help someone else. It was a "pay it forward" movement, so that some good could come out of something that was so bad. Somehow Rich and Samantha and their family found the power to carry on.

There is no greater personal devastation than to lose someone you love. Rich said, "When you lose a child, you always carry that pain." In Acts 1 the disciples of Jesus are about to face the devastation of loss for a second time. They already have lost Jesus once. Jesus died a horrible death and was buried in a borrowed tomb. The disciples' hope was gone. But then something amazing happened. Jesus was raised from the dead, and their hope was restored.

For 40 days, Jesus presented himself alive, appearing to his disciples and speaking about the kingdom of God. But now, they were about to lose him a second time. Jesus was about to be taken up to heaven, and he would be gone from their sight. No longer would he be present so they could see him. I can only imagine how the disciples must have felt. They must have wondered how they could possibly carry on without him. They asked if his imminent departure meant the imminent arrival of God's kingdom. In other words, did his leaving them mean that the world was coming to an end? If not, would life somehow go on? And if life did go on, how would they go on without him?

Jesus said, in essence, "It's not for you to know when the Father will bring in his kingdom in all its fullness." But until that time comes, "you will receive power when the Holy Spirit comes upon you, and you will be my witnesses in Jerusalem, and in all Judea and Samaria, and to the ends of the earth." And after he had said this, Jesus was lifted up, and a cloud took him out of their sight.

We call it the Ascension, and many churches celebrate Ascension Sunday. But the story is about more than Jesus going to heaven, to his rightful place with the Father. It's also about those left behind, who once again were facing a devastating loss. They needed power to carry on. And Jesus promised that they would receive power when the Holy Spirit came upon them. Then they would be his witnesses to the ends of the earth.

This story says to me that there is hope even after devastating loss. God does not leave us powerless when someone we love is taken from us. God sends the Holy Spirit to comfort us, to empower us to carry on, and to live faithful lives for him. It certainly wasn't easy for the disciples after Jesus left. They had to find their way without him. But they stayed together, and they prayed together, and eventually they were filled with the power of the Holy Spirit. It certainly wasn't easy for the Specht family after the death of their young son, but something positive has come out of that tragedy. Somehow God is able to transform even tragic losses and bring good out of them.

Rich Specht received an email from someone he did not know. He almost didn't open the email because he didn't recognize the sender. But for some reason he had a feeling that he should read the message. The email was from a waitress who worked in a Manhattan restaurant. Attached to the email was a photo of a receipt that she had processed at the Times Square restaurant. The amount of the meal was just over $43, but the remarkable thing about the receipt was the amount of the tip: $3,000. No, it wasn't a mistake. The diner deliberately left her a $3,000 tip.

The diner was a regular customer in the restaurant, and he knew the server well. He was an up-and-coming performer on Broadway, and she had taken an interest in his career. He learned that she was having financial difficulties, so he left the incredibly generous tip as a "random act of kindness" to help her out in her time of need. On the back of the receipt, the incredibly generous diner wrote a message to the server. He asked her to do three things: First, check out the ReesSpecht Life website. Second, pass on a "random act of kindness" to someone else. Third, avoid giving out their names should she decide to share what had happened.

When Rich Specht read the email, he recognized the diner as one of his former students. Rich had taught the young man when he was in 8th grade. Rich had not heard from him since. But when the former student, now a rising Broadway star, heard about the tragedy that his middle-school science teacher had suffered, he was inspired to do something to help someone else. The $3,000 tip was given in memory of the little boy who had drowned in the backyard pond. And the gift goes on.[1]

I don't know anything about the religious faith of the Broadway performer, who is still anonymous, and I don't know about the religious beliefs of Rich and Samantha Specht. But I do know that God gives us power to do good. That's what the power of the Holy Spirit is about—the power to do good. Jesus said, "you will receive power when the Holy Spirit has come upon you, and you will be my witnesses…to the ends of the earth." We are witnesses for Christ when we do good in his name, when we share his love with those around us. We are witnesses for Christ when we tell of the hope that is ours through our faith in him.

Jesus was lifted up, and a cloud took him out of the disciples' sight. Those who loved him could have felt lost at losing Jesus yet again. Instead, they stayed together, and they prayed together, and they were filled with the power of the Holy Spirit. And in the power of the Holy Spirit, the followers of Jesus began to change the world.

On Pentecost Sunday we celebrate the gift of the Holy Spirit, but we don't have to wait until Pentecost for the power to come upon us. If you believe in Jesus, the power of the Holy Spirit is available in your life right now. It's a power that can help you to overcome whatever loss you have experienced. It's a power than can help you to transform that loss into a gain, to bring something good out of something bad.

Rich Specht says that when he and his wife set up the foundation to honor their son, they never imagined it would have such an impact. But in the years since Rees died, countless acts of kindness have been performed in his name. More than 750,000 of those ReesSpecht Life cards are now in circulation around the globe. And the gift goes on.

You will receive power when the Holy Spirit comes upon you. If you believe in Jesus, the Holy Spirit is present in your life even now. You have the power. What will you do?

QUESTIONS FOR DISCUSSION/REFLECTION

1. Have you ever had a time in your life when you felt the absence of Christ?
2. What does it mean to you to be filled with the Holy Spirit?
3. How can you help take the gospel to the ends of the earth?
4. Baptism is a "now what?" moment for the believer. Is there a "now what?" moment in your life at the present time?
5. How are you using the power of the Holy Spirit in your life?

NOTE

[1] http://specht.littlethings.com/man-leaves-3000-dollar-tip/rees-tip.

CHAPTER 2

THE HOLY SPIRIT
(Acts 2:1-4)

> *When Pentecost Day arrived, they were all together in one place. Suddenly a sound from heaven like the howling of a fierce wind filled the entire house where they were sitting. They saw what seemed to be individual flames of fire alighting on each one of them. They were all filled with the Holy Spirit and began to speak in other languages as the Spirit enabled them to speak.*
>
> (Acts 2:1-4 CEB)

It is one of the most familiar and most amazing stories in the Bible. We talk about it every year on Pentecost Sunday. Pentecost was originally a Jewish holy day. The Jewish tradition said that the law had been given seven weeks, or about 50 days, after Passover. Pentecost was a time when Jews from all over the Mediterranean world would make a pilgrimage to Jerusalem to celebrate the holy festival. But after what happened to the followers of Jesus on the day of Pentecost, it became an important Christian holy day.

The Holy Spirit descended upon them like tongues of fire and filled all of them. John the Baptist had promised that One was coming who would baptize with the Holy Spirit and with fire (Luke 3:16). Before his ascension, the Risen Jesus had promised that the Holy Spirit would come upon them (Acts 1:8). About a week after Jesus ascended, it happened. The gift of the Holy Spirit empowered the followers of Jesus to speak in other languages—a reversal of the tower of Babel story in Genesis 11. It was the beginning of the followers of Jesus being his witnesses to the ends of the earth.

THE GIFT OF THE HOLY SPIRIT
(Acts 2:1-4, 37-39)

Back in 1991, I was granted the degree of Master of Arts in Counseling Psychology from Bowie State University. Although I was serving full-time as a pastor, I went back to school part-time to sharpen my counseling skills. The Counseling Psychology degree at Bowie State was offered in conjunction with the Washington Pastoral Counseling Service. During my final year in the program, I worked as a part-time pastoral counselor with the Prince George's Pastoral Counseling Service, where I had previously served on the board of directors. I completed my classroom studies, research project, and field experiences on my own time. This was before I took up golf, so I devoted my Thursdays to scholarly pursuits rather than hitting a little white ball all over the golf course.

One of my textbooks was a massive volume with the daunting title, *Diagnostic and Statistical Manual of Mental Disorders, 3rd Edition, Revised*—or DSM-IIIR for short. Shortly after I graduated, DSM-IV was published, updating and revising DSM-IIIR. Then some 20 years later came DSM-5, published by the American Psychiatric Association. Here in America, the DSM is like the "bible" of mental health practitioners. Psychiatrists, psychologists, clinical social workers, therapists, counselors, and other mental health professionals use the *Diagnostic and Statistical Manual* to diagnose mental disorders.

Since DSM-5 was the first major revision in nearly 20 years, there was a bit of controversy after its release. Some diagnoses had been removed, such as "Asperger's syndrome," which was subsumed under "autism spectrum disorder." Some diagnoses had been added, such as "hoarding disorder." The list of mental disorders is constantly changing because our definition of what is "normal" and what is "abnormal" is constantly changing. The current edition of the DSM lists some 157 specific mental disorders. Two disorders were deleted, and 15 were added.

Diagnosing a mental disorder can sometimes help explain why people do what they do, and hopefully can help mental health professionals do a better job of taking care of their clients and patients. The goal, of course, is to help people get better. But not every aberration in human behavior can be explained by a mental disorder. Sometimes people choose to act in unsocial or hurtful ways.

It is difficult to explain what possessed a man in Cleveland to kidnap three young females off the street and hold them captive in his home for almost a decade. The young women were kidnapped between 2002 and 2004 and held as captives in the man's house until 2013. What that man did to those young women defies any kind of rational explanation. Even more troubling is that he seemed to be fairly normal. No one suspected such deviant behavior. (For crying out loud, he drove a school bus for 20 years!) There were a few signs of trouble, however.

Years before, he had been charged with domestic abuse against his common-law wife, but the case was dropped. Apparently, she refused to press charges. Eventually he was fired from his job as a school bus driver, after a series of reprimands. Neighbors saw him taking his 6-year-old daughter to the playground, but they didn't see anything that made them particularly suspicious. He was well-known as a part-time musician with various bands. Apparently not even his relatives suspected he was holding three women hostage in his basement, much less that he was beating and sexually assaulting and abusing and terrorizing them over the course of 10 years. It is shocking that something like that could go on so long and no one noticed anything out of the ordinary.

There is often an element of mystery as to why people do what they do. No doubt, someone might suggest that some childhood trauma or other mental disorder caused the kidnapper's monstrous behavior. Still, it baffles the mind to understand how someone who acted so normal in public could do such horrendous acts behind closed doors. If the guy really did have a mental disorder, he did quite a job of concealing it.

The Bible offers another explanation for what happened in Cleveland. It is called sin. It is called yielding to temptation or giving in to evil. Clearly this guy knew that what he was doing was wrong. That's why he went to such great lengths to hide it.

Temptation is a part of life. Even Jesus was tempted to do the wrong thing. That's why he taught his disciples to pray: "Lead us not into temptation but deliver from evil." Jesus knew that anyone and everyone could be tempted to do the wrong thing. He knew there is a spirit of evil in this world that all too often entices people to go the wrong way. It is part of the free will that God has given us. God wants us to obey him and follow him and do the right thing, but God does not force us to be good. We have a choice. There are all kinds of influences in our lives—some good and some bad—and we choose which influences will have sway over us.

Some years ago, during a children's story time at my church, Leslie Parreco gave a demonstration using two unopened cans of soda. One was a regular soda, and the other a diet soda. The regular soda contained sugar. The diet soda contained an artificial sweetener. Leslie took the regular soda can and lowered it into a glass container filled with water. The regular can of soda sank to the bottom of the container because the sugar in it made it heavier than water. Then Leslie placed the diet soda can into the same container of water. The diet soda didn't sink to the bottom. It floated because it didn't have all that sugar in it. Leslie used that demonstration to show the difference between the regular soda and the diet soda. It's not a difference that you could see. Poured into a glass, both types of soda looked the same. But the soda with all the sugar in it was heavier than the diet soda.

I don't know if any of the kids were impressed by that demonstration, but I was. I decided that day to stop drinking regular sodas because I did not need all the sugar that was in them. I was influenced by Leslie's demonstration. Leslie did not force me to switch to diet soft drinks. I still had free will to choose what kind of soda I would drink. But the influence of her demonstration led me to choose to switch to diet soft drinks. Her demonstration also influenced me to choose to drink less sodas, even less diet sodas, and to drink more water instead.

All of us are influenced every day in the choices we make. There is a spirit of evil in this world that can influence us to make the wrong choice. That's why we pray to God to "lead us not into temptation but deliver us from evil." But as Christians we also have a powerful, positive influence in our lives: the gift of the Holy Spirit.

Act 2 tells what happened on the Day of Pentecost after Jesus was resurrected from the dead. It was seven weeks after Easter, and the Risen Christ was no longer present in a visible way. But Jesus had promised to send his Holy Spirit to be present when he no longer was seen.

On the day of Pentecost, which was a Jewish festival held 50 days after Passover, the followers of Jesus were together in one place. Suddenly from heaven there came a sound like a rush of wind. Divided tongues as of fire rested on each one of them—not literal tongues of fire, but that was the best way they could describe it, by analogy, "as" of fire. All of them were filled with the Holy Spirit, and they began to speak in other languages, as the Spirit gave them the ability. Jews from all over the Mediterranean world had come to Jerusalem for the Pentecost festival, and each one heard the followers of Jesus talking about Jesus in language they could understand. Finally, Peter got up and addressed the whole crowd and explained that this gift of the Holy Spirit was the fulfillment of an ancient prophecy.

When the crowd heard Peter's sermon they were cut to the heart. They asked Peter and the other apostles, "What should we do?" Peter replied, "Repent, and be baptized every one of you in the name of Jesus so that your sins may be forgiven; and you will receive the gift of the Holy Spirit." Do you catch that? The gift of the Holy Spirit was not just given to those followers of Jesus who had known him when he was present on the earth. The gift of the Holy Spirit was for everyone who would repent of their sins and be baptized on their faith in Jesus, whether they had ever seen him in person or not. In other words, God gives the Holy Spirit to everyone who believes in Jesus and is baptized on the basis of that faith.

What then does it mean to have the gift of the Holy Spirit? Does it mean that you will live a perfect life? Obviously not! No one is perfect but God alone. Does it mean that you will never sin? Again, no! We still have free will. God gives us the Holy Spirit, but God does not force us to follow him. But the gift of the Holy Spirit becomes a positive influence in our lives, an influence powerful enough to counter the influence of the spirit of evil in our world. In other words, with the gift of the Holy Spirit, we have the power to live faithful Christian lives.

In his children's book, *Oh, the Places You'll Go*, Dr. Seuss wrote,

You have brains in your head. You have feet in your shoes.
You can steer yourself any direction you choose.
You're on your own. And you know what you know.
And YOU are the one who'll decide where to go...

It's true. We are the ones who decide where we will go. We are the ones who choose how we will live. But we are not totally on our own. The Holy Spirit can lead us, if we choose to be led. The Holy Spirit does not force us to follow God, but the Holy Spirit inspires us to follow God and to do the right thing. The gift of the Holy Spirit is ours to receive as we place our faith in Christ. And as we allow the Holy Spirit to inspire us to live for God, our lives will bear the fruit of that Spirit. In Galatians 5:22 Paul wrote, "the fruit of the Spirit is love, joy, peace, patience, kindness, generosity, faithfulness, gentleness, and self-control."

If that man in Cleveland had been inspired by the Holy Spirit, he never would have kidnapped or hurt those young women. Instead, he was influenced by the spirit of evil, and he inflicted untold suffering upon those women and their families and the little girl that one of his victims bore. After he was arrested and charged, he pled guilty and was sentenced to life in prison without the possibility of parole. One month into his sentence, he died from suicide in his prison cell. We can only pray that the Holy Spirit continues to help those victims to heal and to recover from the trauma of their captivity, and to finally be allowed to live their lives on their own terms. And we can pray that we will be guided by the Holy Spirit, that we might choose to bear the fruit of the Spirit in our own lives. Come, Holy Spirit: fill us with your love.

FILLED WITH THE SPIRIT
(Acts 2:1-4)

We were curious. Three seminary classmates and I wanted to see what being "filled with the Spirit" was all about. None of us had ever been to a Pentecostal church. None of us had ever seen faith healing in person. None of us had ever heard people speaking in tongues in person. So, when we saw an ad for a "Spirit-filled" revival in a church on the other side of town, we were curious. And so, we went.

The main attraction was the guest preacher—a 6-year-old traveling evangelist. As it turned out, the 6-year-old's father did a lot of the talking, but the little tyke did preach a very animated sermon. Then he called people to come forward to be healed. As people lined up facing the platform, the boy laid his hands on them, and some of them were "slain in the Spirit," and they fell to the floor in an almost trance-like state. While this was going on, the organist and the electric guitar player and the drummer played loud gospel music to a pulsating beat. Others in the congregation began dancing in the aisles, and some began speaking in tongues.

The four of us sat near the back of the room in wide-eyed amazement. We were dumbfounded that people could be worked into such an emotional frenzy by a child barely old enough to read and by music with little more than a strong bass beat to it. We did not understand that it was not the child evangelist or the rhythm of the music that made people react as they did. It was the expectations of the worshippers. They came expecting to have a Spirit-filled experience. They came expecting to be moved to dance or to swoon or to speak in tongues. The four of us did not have that kind of experience that night because we did not have that kind of expectation. We came as curious observers, and we left still puzzled over what being "filled with the Spirit" was all about.

Please do not think that I am disparaging our Christian brothers and sisters who worship in Pentecostal churches. Those charismatic churches that emphasize the gifts of the Spirit, the charisma, have a scriptural basis for their beliefs. They go back to the day of Pentecost, when the Holy Spirit came upon the first Christians in a new and powerful way.

There is a scriptural warrant for the gifts of the Spirit. But it is possible to be a "pentecostal" Christian without speaking in tongues. It is possible to be "filled with the Spirit" without worshipping in a charismatic way. In fact, the phenomenon at that first Pentecost was not *glossolalia* at all. When the disciples began to speak in other languages, they could be understood. It was not the unintelligible speech that we now call "speaking in tongues." The whole point of their ability to speak in other languages was so that people could understand what they were saying. Being filled with the Spirit enabled them to communicate the good news of Jesus.

Still, this whole business of being filled with the Spirit sounds rather strange and mysterious to us—almost weird. We are suspicious of religion that gets too emotional, or leads people to seemingly lose control of themselves, or expects people to check their powers of reasoning at the door. But as I read the Bible, that is not what being filled with the Spirit really means. How do you describe something so ethereal as the Holy Spirit?

In Acts 2, Luke says that it was like the rush of a mighty wind and tongues of fire. In the Old Testament, both wind and fire were used as symbols for the presence of God. In Hebrew and in Greek, the words for "wind" and "spirit" are the same. The Hebrew word is *ruah*, which can be translated as either "wind" or "spirit." The Greek word is *pneuma*, which also can be translated as "wind" or "spirit." So, the Spirit of God is comparable to wind and fire. The Spirit of God is a mighty power that comes into our lives—an inner force, an internal energy. We cannot describe the Holy Spirit in literal terms, just as we cannot describe God in literal terms. But what we can say is that the Spirit is like wind or like fire.

Notice that being filled with the Spirit was a community experience. This was not an individual experience that happened only to a select few who had achieved an elevated level of piety or holiness. It happened to all the followers of Jesus after they came together for fellowship and prayer. This was a corporate experience that happened to the whole band of believers. The scripture says, "and all were filled with the Holy Spirit."

In our culture, we tend to privatize religion. We tend to make religion a matter of personal and individual belief. Some people have the notion that you can be a Christian without being a part of any church. Some people believe that you can be a Christian in isolation, apart from the fellowship of other believers. They imagine that faith is a strictly private matter between the individual and God. But the New Testament knows nothing of this "Lone Ranger" mentality. In the New Testament, Christians are always in relationship with other Christians. It was unthinkable for a person to profess faith in Christ and not be part of the church.

You probably have heard the African proverb, "It takes a whole village to raise a child." In the same way, it takes a whole church to raise a Christian. A person who accepts Christ and then tries to live a Christian life in isolation from the church and other Christians misunderstands the nature of our faith. It was Jesus who first formed a community of believers when he gathered a band of disciples. After Jesus departed from them in bodily form, the believers continued to meet together to support one another. And just as Jesus held the disciples together while he was with them on earth, so the Holy Spirit was given to hold the believers together after Jesus was no longer with them in a bodily way.

A farmer in Bruno, Nebraska needed to relocate his barn. He could have torn it down, board by board, and then rebuilt it in its new location. But he came upon a better idea. He decided to pick up the whole barn and move it in one piece. To do that, he enlisted the help of 328 of his friends and neighbors, virtually the entire town of Bruno. After using hydraulic jacks to lift the barn off the ground, all the people gathered around it, took hold, and walked slowly to the new location, 110 feet away. The farmer estimated that working together, each person carried about 50 pounds.

What a wonderful image of the church—people working together to carry a load that no one could do on their own. Every person who is part of the church has something to contribute. The point is: if you want to be filled with the Spirit, get involved in the life of the church. That's how it happened for the first believers. They were already together when the Holy Spirit came upon them. Jesus had promised that they would receive the gift of the Spirit, and they made themselves available. As someone has said, God wants not just our ability, but our availability. And the amazing thing is that when we make ourselves available to God, the Spirit fills our lives in a new and powerful way.

How do you know when you have the Holy Spirit? If you are a Christian, if you have accepted Jesus as your Savior and committed your life to him, you have it. It was on the day of Pentecost that the first Christians became aware of the Holy Spirit in their lives. Pentecost marked the transition from their dependence on Jesus in the flesh to their dependence on Jesus in the Spirit. From that point on, when someone became a Christian, that person received the Holy Spirit. It still happens that way today.

If you are a committed Christian, the Holy Spirit is present in your life. Some people become aware of the presence of the Holy Spirit when they surrender their lives to Christ. Others become aware of the Holy Spirit when they are baptized. For some Christians, it is in looking back on some experience that they realize God's Spirit was with them. However we become aware of God's presence, we can be sure that God is with us through the Holy Spirit.

A middle-aged woman and her elderly father shared a summer home situated on a small lake. One day they decided to take a hike around the lake, both for the exercise and to enjoy the beauties of nature. They began their stroll in mid-afternoon, but along the way they lost track of time. They were about halfway around the lake when they realized that it would soon be dark, and they could not make it back home before sunset. Just then they came across two small boats at the water's edge—a rowboat and a sailboat.

The father suggested they borrow one of the boats and use it go straight across the lake to their house on the other side. Then, they could bring the boat back the next morning and continue their hike around the lake. His daughter agreed this was a good plan, but there was one question. She asked her father, "Which boat should we take?" He replied: "Before I answer that question, let me ask you a question. Is there any wind?" Sure enough, a breeze was blowing. They took the sailboat and soon reached the other side.

Life is similar to a lake, and our home is on the other side. We could choose the rowboat and try to reach the other shore using only our own efforts. Or, we could choose the sailboat and let the winds of God fill our sails and carry us along to that place of welcome and rest.

Is there any wind? For those who believe in Christ, the winds of God are always blowing. A rowboat or a sailboat: which will it be?

ONE IN THE SPIRIT
(Acts 2:1-21)

In 2005 Linda and I traveled with our friends Michele and Mark Miles to Birmingham, England for the World Congress of the Baptist World Alliance. It was like a gathering of the United Nations of Baptists. Every five years Baptists from all over the world come together somewhere for a general meeting. The meetings rotate from continent to continent. The 2005 Baptist World Congress was held in Birmingham, England; the 2010 Congress in Honolulu, Hawaii; and the 2015 Congress in Durban, South Africa.

Linda and I were blessed to attend all three of those meetings, but it is the 2005 Baptist World Congress I tell you about here.

After we checked into our hotel, we were tired from our overnight flight to London and the drive to Birmingham, but we also were incredibly excited. It was thrilling to be among Christians from so many different places. Michele and Mark crashed in their hotel room, but Linda and I were hungry, so we scouted out some place to eat.

We walked over to the conference center and ran into our friend Jere Allen, the former executive director/minister of the D.C. Baptist Convention. Wouldn't you know it? The first person we would meet in England was a guy I played golf with every Thursday back home. Jere pointed us to a restaurant, and we got some dinner. On our way back to the hotel, we passed groups of Baptists from Africa and Asia and South America and Europe. We even saw some other Americans. We could guess where people were from by the way they were dressed.

The Baptist World Congress began the next day. The Birmingham Convention Center was packed with thousands of people. I looked for familiar faces in the crowd, but with so many people from all over the world, I wondered if we would ever again run into someone we knew.

I was riding up an escalator when I heard a voice call out my name. It was Champion Chasara from Zimbabwe, who had visited our church in Maryland on two occasions. I jumped off at the top of the escalator and took the down escalator to a joyful reunion with our dear friend. Over the course of the next few days, there were many such reunions. We ran into Kingsley Perrera, a Baptist leader from Sri Lanka, who also had visited our church a few years before. We saw most of the Cooperative Baptist Field Personnel who had visited our church—Tammy and Ralph Stocks from Hungary, Keith Holmes and Mary van Rheenen from the Netherlands, Macarena and Eddie Aldape from India, along with former missionaries Kathie and T Thomas, and Jane and Earl Martin.

One evening during the Congress, the Miles and the Salmons took a group of our friends from Zimbabwe to dinner. There were 10 of us altogether, including Champion and his daughter Margaret, another couple from Champion's church and their niece, and the general secretary of the Baptist Convention of Zimbabwe, John Mazvigadza, who also had visited my church in Maryland. What a joy it was to meet new friends and to spend time with old ones!

On another day, during a luncheon honoring former President Jimmy Carter, we sat at a table with a couple from Indonesia. The wife did not speak English, but her husband was a retired Indonesian Air Force officer who had trained in the U.S. He had become a Christian through the influence of a Baptist missionary in Indonesia, and through his exposure to Christian Air Force officers here in America.

In addition to meeting people from other nations, we heard musical groups from many countries—singers and dancers from Nagaland in northeast India, folk singers and guitarists from Chile, choirs from South Africa and the Czech Republic, a children's choir from South Korea, and a rock band from the Congo. Sometimes they sang in English; sometimes they sang in their own language. We didn't understand every word, but the gospel message always came through.

The day of Pentecost in Jerusalem was like a gathering of the United Nations of God's people. Citizens from many different countries had come together for the holy festival. Some were Jews by birth. Others were proselytes drawn to the Jewish religion because of its belief in one God and its high ethical standards. It was an incredibly diverse and international gathering. Those present spoke many languages, but as the disciples were filled with the Holy Spirit, each person heard the gospel preached in her or his own native tongue. It was like a reversal of the tower of Babel.

The apostle Peter explained this phenomenon as the fulfillment of prophecy. According to the prophet Joel, in the messianic age God would pour out his Spirit on all believers. Previously, God's Spirit had been given only to special people such as Moses, David, Elijah, John the Baptist, and Jesus. But now the gift of God's Spirit would be available to everyone. Peter said, "Repent and be baptized every one of you in the name of Jesus Christ so that your sins may be forgiven; and you will receive the gift of the Holy Spirit" (Acts 2:38).

Pentecost was the day when the Holy Spirit was given to everyone who believed in Jesus. Peter promised that from then on, everyone who would repent and believe in Jesus and be baptized would receive the gift of the Holy Spirit too. In 1 Corinthians 3:16 Paul wrote, "Do you not know that you are God's temple, and that God's Spirit dwells in you?" This means that every Christian is a temple of the Holy Spirit. Later, Paul would write about the fruits of the Spirit—meaning the positive results of allowing God's Spirit to work in and through us—qualities such as love, joy, peace, patience, kindness, goodness, faithfulness, gentleness, and self-control (Gal. 5:22-23). The Holy Spirit is the power that God gives all believers to live faithful Christian lives. In addition, the Holy Spirit unites Christians into one body—namely the church. We are one in the Spirit because the Holy Spirit makes us one.

Because we Christians are one in the Spirit, Linda and I were so happy to see our friends from Zimbabwe: we are one with each other through our faith in Jesus. Apart from our common faith in Christ, it is unlikely that we ever would have met those people from Zimbabwe, much less become friends with them. But because we share a common faith in Jesus, and because we have received the gift of the Holy Spirit, we are united in a way that transcends divisions of race or national origins or other circumstances of life. This means that if you believe in Jesus, you and I are one in the Spirit. It doesn't matter where we come from or what our racial ancestry may be or what is our status in life, we are connected by the Spirit of God.

The first church was an incredibly diverse collection of believers, made up of people from all parts of the then-known world. They spoke different languages, followed different customs, and wore different styles of clothing, but they were one in the Spirit, because the Holy Spirit made them one. We are one in the Spirit because we believe in Jesus, and the Holy Spirit makes us one.

My experiences at the Baptist World Congress in England in 2005, in Hawaii in 2010, and in South Africa in 2015 were all powerful reminders that we are one in the Spirit. May the love of God, and the grace of our Lord Jesus Christ, and the fellowship of the Holy Spirit truly make us one.

QUESTIONS FOR DISCUSSION/REFLECTION

1. How would you explain to a non-Christian the gift of the Holy Spirit?
2. What power has the Holy Spirit given you?
3. What can we do to accentuate our unity through the Spirit?
4. How does your life show that you are filled with the Spirit?
5. How can you be guided by the Holy Spirit in your day-to-day life?

CHAPTER 3

THE SEVEN
(Acts 6:1-6)

> *But as the believers rapidly multiplied, there were rumblings of discontent... "We apostles should spend our time... teaching the word of God, not administering a food program... select seven men who are well respected and are full of the Holy Spirit and wisdom. We will put them in charge of this business. Then we apostles can spend our time in prayer and preaching and teaching the word."*
>
> (Acts 6:1a, 2b, 3b-4 NLT)

We might call this episode in Acts 6 "the first church fight." It was not exactly a knock-down, drag-out brawl, but there was disagreement, and likely, some hurt feelings. The issue was the church's benevolence ministry. Some church members thought it was not being distributed fairly. There was a cultural, perhaps even racial, component to the dispute. Greek-speaking church members felt that their needy widows were being slighted when it came to the daily distribution of food. So, the 12 apostles called a church business meeting, and a committee was chosen to oversee the program; the disciples could then focus on preaching and teaching.

The seven committee members were all from the Hellenist community, and one was even a Gentile convert. They did far more than "wait tables." Stephen was an eloquent and powerful evangelist, whose prophesying led to his martyrdom (Acts 7). Philip also became an evangelist who took the gospel to Samaria, and then, on his way to Gaza, converted and baptized an Ethiopian eunuch (Acts 8). The seven were commissioned to administer the food ministry and to assist in leading the growing Christian community. Traditionally, the seven are regarded as the first deacons of the church, although they functioned more like bishops or presbyters. Most importantly, they helped the church stay together in the aftermath of what could have been a divisive controversy.

CHOSEN TO SERVE
(Acts 6:1-7)

In the United States we have an election every couple of years—or even more often. Some years we vote for local officials or representatives to Congress. Every four years we vote for president. Elections are important because they determine who will lead us, and who will serve us. Acts 6 tells of an election in the church in Jerusalem, one that came out of a crisis in the church. A dispute arose about how the benevolence program of the church was being administered.

In that time, before Social Security or any kind of government assistance, widows were particularly vulnerable. A woman who did not have a husband to provide for her might go hungry. So, to take care of the widows in the congregation, the church provided a daily distribution of food. The problem was that this daily distribution of food was not equitable. Some Hellenist, Greek-speaking members of the church complained that their widows were being neglected.

To understand how this could have happened, we need to understand the diversity of the church in Jerusalem. They were all Jewish Christians, but they were Jews from two different backgrounds. The Palestinian Jews had grown up around Jerusalem and spoke Aramaic. They probably were more religiously conservative, because they lived in the shadow of the Temple and were surrounded with elements of the Jewish religion, such as super-observant Pharisees and priests. The Hellenistic Jews came from regions far beyond Palestine and spoke Greek. They were probably less conservative in their approach and were not as concerned with maintaining all the religious customs that the Palestinian Jews considered important.

This division of language and custom led to discrimination within the Jerusalem church. The Hebrew widows received their full measure of the daily distribution of food, but the Hellenist widows were shortchanged, and some may have been in danger of going hungry. So, there was discrimination in the church. This led to a crisis that threatened to disrupt the fellowship and hinder the spread of the gospel.

The 12 apostles, who were the leaders of the church in Jerusalem at this early stage, recognized the severity of the crisis. Rather than taking it upon themselves to oversee the daily distribution of food, and thereby neglect their other duties, the apostles called for an election. They said, "select from among yourselves seven men of good standing, full of the Spirit and of wisdom, whom we may appoint to this task" (Acts 6:3). All seven who were elected had Greek names, suggesting that they were Greek-speaking and therefore would ensure that the Hellenist widows would not be neglected in the daily distribution of food. The seven were well-chosen. The crisis was resolved, and the word of God continued to spread. The number of disciples increased greatly in Jerusalem, and even a great many priests became obedient to the faith.

From this story we see that discrimination has always been a threat to Christian unity. For the church in Jerusalem, it was not strictly racial discrimination, for all the members of the early church in Jerusalem were Jews (although at least one of the seven was a Gentile convert). There was also discrimination based on language and culture.

Here in America, racial discrimination in the church has been much more overt. In many communities, even today, churches are still largely racially segregated. Truly diverse churches are a novelty in many places. When I first became pastor of our church in Maryland, we had only a handful of African-American members. This changed gradually, so that by the time I retired after 33 years at the church, our congregation was roughly 50/50, black and white. That transition was possible because our church was in a truly integrated community, and because the members of our church sought to welcome everyone.

To be honest, diversity is not always easy to maintain. Many churches struggle to maintain unity in diversity. My mother's church in Texas went through a crisis over the issue of same-sex couples. When the church was going to publish a new pictorial directory, some same-sex couples wanted to be pictured as families. Some members of the congregation were okay with that, but others were not, and it ended up splitting the church. Some members left, including some of her friends, and eventually even the pastor left. It was a very divisive issue that disrupted the unity of the church. Sooner or later, most churches will have to deal with this issue. Do we make it a "my way or the highway" decision, or can we agree to respectfully disagree and remain united in love as a family of faith?

Roy Medley served 14 years as the general secretary of the American Baptist Churches USA. When asked his opinion on the state of the church and what can be done to reach people who have no religious affiliation (the "nones") and those who have left the church (the "dones"), Dr. Medley replied:

> Reaching the "nones" and "dones" is one of the challenges the church faces in North America. Our basic message needs to be that which is has always been: "God loves you." Many young adults I speak with ask why the church has to be so judgmental and condemning. We need to quit emphasizing what we are "anti" and instead promote what we are "for." They wish to meet a people who mirror the compassion of Jesus.[1]

What impresses me about the believers in the church in Jerusalem is not that they avoided controversy, but that they worked their way through it. Despite their differences, they managed to stay together by putting the needs of each other above their personal preferences. They recognized that everyone in the church was of value, however different, and that everyone should be treated fairly. So, they had an election to select seven Spirit-filled leaders who would help restore trust in the congregation.

Ultimately, the church is in the people business. We are in the business of mirroring the love and compassion of Jesus and maintaining unity in diversity. We express our faith in Jesus most definitively by the way we treat other people. Jesus said the two greatest commandments are to love God and to love our neighbors as we love ourselves.

I was honored to give the invocation for a member of my church, Ron, at his retirement ceremony from the federal government after 36½ years of service. In his last position, he served an agency with about 20,000 federal employees under his leadership. During the ceremony Ron was presented with awards and commendations by many distinguished government leaders. But the most impressive part of the ceremony for me was when Ron asked his former executive assistants to join him at the front of the room. There must have been more than a dozen of them who came forward. Each one greeted Ron with a handshake, a hug, a smile, and some words of appreciation. It was clear that these were not scripted responses, but instead spontaneous expressions of affection and respect. Ron had been their boss, but he was more than their boss. He was their mentor; he was someone they admired and looked up to. The fact that Ron wanted to recognize his executive assistants during his retirement ceremony helped explain their feelings for him.

Ron may have worked for the federal government, but he was in the people business. He expressed his faith in God by the way he treated other people. Of course, I and other members of my church already knew that about Ron. He and his wife were active members, and Ron served as a deacon. But I was impressed to see that same side of Ron in his professional life.

The way we treat other people is an expression of our faith. What we say we believe is important, but how we live out what we believe is even more important. Personal relationships are where we see faith in action. Whenever we elect church leaders, we pray that they will help us to mirror the compassion of Jesus, and to share the love of God with everyone. In a way, all of us have been chosen to serve. If we mirror the love of Jesus, the word of God will spread, and the number of disciples will increase among us too.

WAITING ON TABLES
(Acts 6:1-7)

When my daughter Amy was home from college one summer, she landed her dream job—working at Pizza Hut. At the time we moved to Bowie, Amy was in middle school, and the closest Pizza Hut was on the north side of town. But the stars had aligned by the time she was in high school: a Pizza Hut had opened in south Bowie in the Pointer Ridge Shopping Center. When Amy was a little girl, whereas some little girls played "tea party," Amy played "Pizza Hut." At first, she was excited to be working at Pizza Hut, but over time the excitement faded. As the dream turned into reality, she found that working at Pizza Hut was not nearly so exciting as her dream.

The reality is that waiting on tables is not a glamorous job, especially not at Pizza Hut. It's not like at a fancy restaurant where servers can make good money with big tips. But even though the reality was not as great as her dream, Amy continued to work at Pizza Hut because she needed the money. She also worked at a department store in Bowie, in the Marketplace shopping center. But Pizza Hut was her dream job. Now, there is nothing wrong with waiting on tables. A lot of people have done it, and some people manage to make a career out of it. But it is not glamourous work. We used to call people who wait on tables "waiters" or "waitresses." Now, the term is "servers." Whatever we call it, the job still involves waiting and serving.

Acts 6 tells of seven men in the church in Jerusalem being elected to wait on tables. It's not that the church was in the restaurant business. But the church was involved in the distribution of food, primarily to widows and others in need. Among the members of the church in Jerusalem, widows were particularly vulnerable. Because there was no Social Security system, no survivor benefits, there was no safety net for women who had lost their husbands. The Old Testament taught that the care of widows was the responsibility of the entire Jewish community. But what about widows who were members of the church? They were looked upon with suspicion by the larger Jewish community. Soon, followers of Jesus were no longer welcome in the synagogues; they would become targets of persecution. So, widows who had become Christians were especially vulnerable. Who would care for them?

This is where the church stepped in to help. There was a daily distribution to aid the widows. Sometimes it was a distribution of food. Sometimes it was a distribution of money to buy food. Either way, this benevolent assistance was crucial to helping those vulnerable widows survive. The problem was that this daily food assistance was not being distributed equitably. Some of the widows were being neglected and going hungry. Something had to be done.

Underlying this problem was a division in the church. The church was divided along cultural and linguistic lines. They were all Jews, but they were two types of Jews. They were all believers in Jesus, but they had come from different backgrounds.

The Hebrews were natives of Jerusalem or Palestine. They spoke the local language, Aramaic, and reflected the conservative culture of their homeland. The Hellenists had emigrated to Jerusalem from other parts of the Roman empire. They spoke Greek and reflected the cosmopolitan culture of other places. Not only did they speak a different language, but it may be that the Hellenists dressed and acted differently than their Hebrew counterparts. A division in the church resulted. They all believed in Jesus, but their languages and lifestyles were different. It came to the attention of the apostles that not everyone in the church was being treated equally. The Hellenist widows were the victims of discrimination.

The apostles were all Palestinian Jews. They identified more with the Hebrew widows than the Hellenist widows. But the apostles recognized that the Hellenist widows were of equal value in the sight of God and therefore should be treated equally in the church. The problem was that the apostles had their hands full with preaching and seeking to advance the gospel. So, they instructed the church to select from among themselves seven men of good standing, full of the Spirit and of wisdom. The apostles would appoint them to "wait on tables," to administer the daily distribution.

The church was to select seven men—it was still a man's world back then. Eventually there would be a few instances where women were recognized as leaders in some of the churches, but not in Jerusalem, at least not then. In the culture of the time, women were still subservient, and dependent on men—hence, the need for men to make sure that the widows were cared for.

The Jerusalem church held an election. The seven men selected to "wait on tables" all had Greek names, indicating they were Hellenists themselves, Greek-speaking Jewish Christians from other parts of the Roman empire. But to think that all they did was "wait on tables" is to grossly underestimate their role. Not only did these seven men organize and supervise the distribution of food to widows in the church, but some of them also became teachers, evangelists, and wonder workers.

For example, one of the seven, Stephen, was a man full of grace and power. Stephen did great wonders and signs among the people. He also was a powerful preacher. One of his sermons is quoted in Acts 7. Stephen was so courageous in his witness for Christ that he became a target of leaders in the synagogue. They stirred up the people against him. The Jews seized him, brought him to the council, and set up false witnesses against him. Eventually they dragged him out of the city and stoned him. One of the Jewish leaders, a Pharisee named Saul, approved of the mob violence against Stephen. In fact, Saul watched over the leaders' cloaks while they threw rocks at Stephen and killed him.

Another of the seven, a man named Philip, also became a great evangelist. As the persecution intensified, many of the church members were scattered throughout the countryside of Judea and Samaria. After burying Stephen, the church members fled.

Saul was going from house to house, arresting any Christians who remained and throwing them into prison. Philip made his way to Samaria, where he boldly preached about Jesus. While there, Philip also performed many miracles—casting out demons, healing the sick. Those who believed in Jesus through Philip's preaching were baptized. Later, Philip was instrumental in the conversion of a man from Ethiopia whom he met on the road to Gaza. Philip led the Ethiopian to faith in Christ and baptized him. So, of the seven who were elected to "wait on tables," at least two of them became courageous evangelists.

The seven selected to "wait on tables" were not called "deacons," but it sounds as if that's what they were. At first, the church in Jerusalem was led by the apostles. Later it was led by James, the brother of Jesus, as the apostles moved on to other places to spread the good news of Jesus. In less than a generation, churches would be planted all over the Roman empire. Each church had leaders. Some of the leaders were called overseers or bishops, and others deacons.

Luke did not use the term "deacon" in the book of Acts. But in the letters of Paul, we read about deacons in Rome and Cenchreae and Philippi. Paul's first letter to Timothy lists the qualifications for deacons. In fact, by the time Paul wrote his letter to Timothy, there seems to have developed two basic categories of church leaders: bishops or overseers, and deacons. Paul wrote in Ephesians about apostles, prophets, evangelists, pastors, and teachers. So, the early churches developed different types of leaders to equip the saints—and "saints" includes all of us—"for the work of ministry, for building up the body of Christ" (Eph. 4:11-12).

All of us are called to serve Christ in some way. We're not all called to be pastors, though some of us are. We're not all called to be deacons, though some of us are. We're not all called to be teachers, or prophets, or evangelists, though some of us are. We're not all called to "wait on tables," though some of us are. For example, a group from my church took some food to the Bowie Church of Christ when that church served as hosts one week for the Warm Nights ministry to the homeless. Then, when Village Baptist Church hosted Warm Nights, other churches helped provide food for our guests. "Waiting on tables" is still an important ministry of the church.

All of us are called to serve Christ in some way. Whatever we are called to do, Jesus said the greatest among us are those who have learned to serve (Luke 22:24-27).

AT YOUR SERVICE
(Acts 6:1-7)

One day I was having lunch with a couple of clergy friends at a local restaurant. The three of us—a Lutheran pastor, a Presbyterian pastor, and a Baptist pastor—were looking over the menu when a young woman approached our table and introduced herself. In the old days, we called such a person a "waitress," but the more politically correct term now is "server." She told us her name, but instead of saying, "I'll be serving you," she said, "I'll be taking care of you."

For some reason, that remark struck my two colleagues as hilarious. They both laughed out loud. One of them said, "Oh, we need someone to take care of us." Perhaps you have to be a pastor to understand the source of our amusement. Even though the three of us came from different denominational backgrounds, we shared a lot of common experiences in our role of being pastor of a church. As pastors, a big part of our job was to take care of people. Among all the helping professionals, pastors are among the preeminent caregivers.

If you try to call a physician outside of regular office hours, you will get an answering service—probably with instructions to go to the emergency room if it is an emergency. If you try to call a counselor or a social worker after hours, you will get a message to call back during office hours and set up an appointment. If you try to call a police officer or a fire fighter, you will get whoever might be on duty at the station at the time. Most health care workers, teachers, and others in the helping professions don't give out their home telephone or cell numbers—so you couldn't call them even if you wanted to. But pastors are different.

We pastors give out our phone numbers, and even though we keep regular office hours, we are always on call. When it comes to taking care of people, I dare say pastors are the most thoroughgoing caregivers. We still make house calls. And unlike persons in the other helping professions, we are not concerned about just one area of a person's life. A health care worker is concerned about your health, a police officer or fire fighter about your safety, a teacher about your education, a counselor your mental health, and a financial advisor about your finances. But pastors are concerned about the totality of a person's life. We may not be able to solve all your problems, but we care about all your problems. It is our calling to care.

The problem with being a caregiver is that it is easy to get burned out. In 2001 a report from the Alban Institute identified a clergy crisis, noting that "a large percentage of professional clergy evidence symptoms of burnout or depression." In the journal *Congregations*, Martin Copenhaver wrote that, "pastors are a beleaguered lot—overburdened and underpaid, overwhelmed and underappreciated."[2] Being on call 24/7, caring deeply about needs and problems beyond our control, can be exhausting. This is not a new phenomenon. It has been the circumstance of church leaders since the beginning.

Acts 6 describes a clergy crisis in the first church in Jerusalem. The church leaders, the apostles, were getting burned out by the demands of their work. They were becoming overwhelmed with the practical responsibilities of caring for the members of the church. In particular, there was a rising complaint among some people in the church that not everyone was being treated fairly. There were tensions along racial lines. Church members from a Greek background felt that the daily distribution of food for widows and others in need favored the Jewish church members.

The apostles found themselves being distracted from their preaching and other spiritual duties in order to get involved in the practical matter of the distribution of food. They recognized they needed help to attend to this ongoing concern. So, the church selected "seven men of good standing, full of the Spirit and of wisdom," to take care of the people who were being neglected. The church set them apart for this special service with prayer and the laying on of hands. The service of these seven freed up the apostles to continue to spread the word of God. As a result, the number of believers increased, and the church continued to grow.

The message of the story in Acts 6 is that the church cannot rely solely on the professional clergy to do its work. Professional clergy preach, teach, pray, counsel, and provide spiritual leadership. But they cannot do it all. Even in a small church, the pastor cannot take care of everyone all the time. The pastor is always on call for special needs, but the pastor needs help. In a sense, everyone in the church, every Christian, is a minister, because God calls each of us to serve in some way.

A family was enjoying a day at the ocean. The children were jumping in the surf and making castles in the sand. Then a frail older lady appeared, slowly walking along the beach. She had a disheveled look about her: her gray hair was blowing in the wind, and her clothes looked plain and rumpled. She was bending down and picking things up and putting them into a tattered shopping bag. The parents called the children over and warned them to stay away from the old woman. She smiled as she passed by, but the family ignored her.

Some weeks later there was an article in the newspaper about the death of a retired schoolteacher. There was a photo with the article, and the mother of the family recognized it was the same woman they had seen walking on the beach that day. The obituary went on to describe the many charitable works this woman had done. It said that she had made it her mission the last years of her life to walk along the beach and pick up bits of glass so that children would not cut their feet on them.

Ordinary people doing simple acts of kindness can make a difference. Everyday deeds of love and service can make the world a better place. The world judges the outside of how a person looks, or what a person has accomplished, or how much a person has accumulated. But God judges the heart. Jesus said that whoever would be great must learn to serve (Matt. 20:26)

QUESTIONS FOR DISCUSSION/ REFLECTION

1. Is some amount of conflict inevitable in the church?
2. What can we do when conflicts arise in the church?
3. What is the best process for selecting church leaders?
4. What is the difference between church leaders and church servants?
5. How do we discern who is "full of the Holy Spirit and wisdom"?

NOTES

[1] ABCUSA *Connections*, Fall 2015.
[2] *Congregations*, September-October, 2001.

CHAPTER 4

RUN THE RACE
(Hebrews 12:1-2)

"Therefore, since we are surrounded by so great a cloud of witnesses, let us also lay aside every weight and the sin that clings so closely, and let us run with perseverance the race that is set before us, looking to Jesus the pioneer and perfecter of our faith, who for the sake of the joy that was set before him he endured the cross, disregarding its shame, and has taken his seat at the right hand of the throne of God."

(Heb. 12:1-2 NRSV)

Hebrews 12:1-2 is the conclusion to Hebrews 11, which is a kind of roll call of the faithful. They are the "cloud of witnesses" who cheer us on as we run the race of faith. Hebrews 11:1 defines faith as "the assurance of things hoped for, the conviction of things not seen."

Races were a familiar sport in the biblical times. In four places in the New Testament, a race is used as a metaphor for the Christian life:

> I have fought the good fight, I have finished the race, I have kept the faith.
> (2 Tim. 4:7)

> Do you not know that in a race the runners all compete,
> but only one receives the prize?
> Run in such a way that you may win it.
> (1 Cor. 9:24)

> I press on toward the goal for the prize of the heavenly call of God in Christ Jesus.
> (Phil. 3:14)

> [L]et us run with perseverance the race that is set before us.
> (Heb. 12:1b)

The event described in Hebrews 12 takes place in a great arena, filled with spectators who are witnessing the race. In this case, the spectators are all the people of faith who have gone before us. They are a great cloud of witnesses who surround us as we run the race that is set before us. Immediately preceding these verses, in Hebrews 11, the author identifies some of those witnesses:

- Abel, who offered a sacrifice more pleasing to God than his brother Cain
- Enoch, who so pleased God that he did not die, but was taken directly into heaven
- Noah, Abraham, Isaac, Jacob, and Joseph
- Moses and the Israelites who passed through the Red Sea during the Exodus from Egypt
- Gideon, Barak, Samson, Jephthah, David, Samuel, and the prophets

Without naming more names, the writer of Hebrews refers to many others who endured mocking and flogging and imprisonment and even martyrdom because of their faith. All these people of faith have gone before us, and they comprise this great cloud of witnesses who are watching us and encouraging us as we run the race that is set before us.

ALL THE WAY HOME
(Heb. 12:1-2, 12-13)

A triathlon is an athletic event that requires phenomenal training, endurance, and strength. It is actually three races, one right after the other. First, the competitors swim in the ocean for 10 miles. That in itself would be enough to do in most of us. After the swim they stagger onto the beach, shake themselves dry, and head for their bicycles. The second part of the triathlon is a 50-mile bike race. Finally, the competitors begin to run. The foot race is 20 miles. Needless to say, the triathlon is one of the most grueling athletic competitions you could imagine. And yet, many incredible athletes, both men and women, have the stamina and the drive and the determination to finish the race.

The author of Hebrews had something like that in mind when he compared the Christian life to a long-distance race, saying that following Jesus is like running in a marathon. If you are to have any hope of finishing, it takes training and endurance and determination and faith. Let me set the scene for you.

In the preceding chapter the author described a pantheon of heroes, a hall of fame, a roll call of men and women who have gone before us as great examples of faith. He listed many of the heroes of the Old Testament—Abel, Enoch, Noah, Abraham, Sarah, Isaac, Jacob, Joseph, Moses, the Israelites crossing the Red Sea, Rahab the harlot, Gideon, Barak, Samson, Jephthah, David, Samuel, the prophets. He called to mind this great galaxy of stars, the procession of the faithful, to challenge us and encourage us and inspire us in our faith in Christ. And now he envisions all those heroes gathered in the stands of a stadium, such as in the Olympics. Can you picture it? Here we are, on the racetrack of a great coliseum, and all around us is that great cloud of witnesses to cheer us on. It almost makes you want to go get your running shoes.

What can we learn from this image of faith in Hebrews? There are several lessons. For one thing, we can learn that the Christian life is a long and difficult race. Don't let anyone kid you: It is hard to follow Christ and to remain faithful to God. It is hard to put the needs of others ahead of your own needs, to turn the other cheek, to go the second mile, to forgive those who do you wrong, to love your enemies. (Sometimes, it is even hard to love your friends or your family!)

Being a Christian is probably the hardest thing you will ever do. Just look at the 12 disciples of Jesus. They were with Jesus all the time, and even they had a hard time following him. They were constantly misunderstanding his teachings. One of them, Judas, betrayed him. The leader of the disciples, Simon Peter, denied Jesus when the pressure was on. After Jesus was arrested, all the disciples ran away. At the foot of the cross, as Jesus was dying, only one disciple, John, dared to show his face. In short, when the chips were down, every disciple was tempted to drop out of the race.

If the disciples, who were with Jesus face-to-face, had a hard time following him, you can be sure it will be hard for us too. This should not surprise us. Things of great value always exact a great price. I don't know anything that is worthwhile in life that is not difficult. It is difficult to sing a song in a beautiful way, to play the organ or the piano well, to preach a good sermon. (It is even difficult to listen to a good sermon!) It is difficult to achieve excellence in your work, to build a happy and healthy home life, to maintain physical vitality and vigor and fitness. Why should we expect our spiritual life to be any different? That's why we emphasize making a Christian commitment. When the going gets tough in our walk with God, it is only those who are absolutely committed to Christ who will see it through. But there's more.

Not only is the Christian life difficult; it is long. We are not talking about a 100-yard dash. The race that the author of Hebrews describes is not a sprint, but a marathon. It is more than walking the aisle and getting baptized. It is more than getting your name on a church roll. It is a race that we will run for the rest of our lives. And if we are going to last through that kind of race, we'll need some help along the way.

If you have watched a marathon race, you have seen that it is essential for the runners to drink water and to take nourishment along the way. Even if they do not feel thirsty, the runners have learned that they must discipline themselves to drink at certain strategic points, or their bodies will collapse from dehydration. And so, as they are running, they will grab a cup of water or some other nourishment and take it to replenish their body fluids. The same applies to the Christian life.

As runners in the race of faith, we also need some replenishment along the way. We need spiritual disciplines such as prayer, Bible study, worship, and Christian fellowship. And yet, it is so easy to slide into a kind of spiritual lethargy. People can get out of the habit of going to church. They miss a week, then two, then a month, and eventually they don't even think about it. It's the same with Bible study and prayer.

Linda and I received a letter from a friend in another state. We had not seen her for several years, but we sent her a Christmas card, and that prompted her to write a very personal letter. In the letter she described what had been happening in her life, including the death of her father. It was a heart-wrenching story. He had cancer, and toward the end he was in physical torment. The doctors gave him the strongest painkillers they had, and still it was not enough. Finally, out of desperation, our friend could do nothing for her father to relieve his pain except sit beside his hospital bed and read from the Bible. She read from Romans 8, about how nothing can separate us from the love of God.

When all else had failed our friend's father in his last days, the Bible was the only medicine that did any real good. The same is true with prayer. There is something in our minds and emotions that needs to center down, to put aside extraneous concerns, to reach out to God.

Another source of spiritual nourishment is Christian fellowship. We can gain strength for the journey from one another. It doesn't matter how long the road stretches before us—the distance will seem shorter if someone else will go along.

When I was a boy in elementary school, my mother often would take me to school in the morning by car, but most days I would walk home after school in the afternoon. It was only a mile or so, but when I walked by myself it seemed like a long way. But if a friend would walk with me, the journey always seemed shorter.

I'm not a schoolboy anymore, but I still walk now and then. And it does make a difference whether I walk alone or with a friend. That's what we're here for. We're here to walk together along life's road. Yes, the race is difficult and long, but there is nourishment—worship, prayer, the Bible, each other—to help along the way.

There is something else we can learn about running the race of faith. We've got to lay aside the weights that would encumber us and hold us back. When they run the triathlon, the competitors strip down to only their essential clothing and shoes. They don't even wear a number on a piece of cloth or a badge to identify themselves. Instead, the number is written on their flesh, on their arms with a felt-tipped marker. They travel as light as possible because they know that any extra weight can mean the difference between finishing and quitting.

It doesn't make sense to run a race with a knapsack full of rocks strapped to your back. Yet, some of us try to do that. Some of us are so weighed down by unnecessary loads that we can hardly run at all. What are some of the weights that slow us down?

Some of us are weighed down by guilt. Maybe we have done some things wrong—who hasn't? Guilt can help us to put things right, but guilt can also weigh us down when we hang onto it. There is a word for us: Accept God's grace and let go of your guilt. Take that stone of guilt out of your backpack and move on.

Some of us are weighed down by worries. We fret about our health or our children or our finances or our work. There is a word for us: Do what you can, and then trust your worries to God. Take that stone of worry out of your bag and move on.

Some of us are burdened by self-pity. Maybe life has dealt us some bad cards. Maybe we have had our share of bad breaks. We can do something about that. We can play the hand that is dealt us, knowing that God works in all circumstances for good. Take that stone of self-pity out of your pack and move on.

Some of us are preoccupied with success. Our sense of self-worth is tied up with how much money we make or what position we hold or how much credit we deserve. But God offers us a different standard of self-worth. We have value in God's eyes, not because of what we can do or what we possess, but simply because of who we are. Let go of that preoccupation with success and move on.

Some of us have made an idol of the past. We cling to some bygone day as though things were perfect back then. They were not. The past can be weight that loads us down and holds us back from the future that God has set before us. Remove that stone and move on.

Hebrews says to us, "lay aside every weight and sin which clings so closely." Lay them aside, empty your knapsack, let them go. If you would finish the race, those extra burdens only get in the way. If guilt or worries or self-pity or success or the past weigh you down, you'll never make it to the end. Accept God's grace and move on.

One more thing about the race of faith—the goal: The scripture says, "let us run with perseverance the race that is set before us, looking to Jesus the pioneer and perfecter of our faith, who for the joy that was set before him endured the cross, despising the shame, and is seated at the right hand of the throne of God." Two goals are set before us—two goals that are really one—Jesus and joy. That is why we run, endure, and journey that long and difficult road of faith. At the end of the road, and even along the way, there is Jesus and there is joy.

The heroes are in the stands as witnesses, and we, you and I, are running the race of faith. And as we run, those saints of old are cheering us on. They're yelling, "Keep going, don't give up, you can make it, you can finish, you can do it!" They are cheering us on to victory. And they should know. They have a right to cheer. They ran the race of faith, they finished the course, and so can we. Where are your running shoes?

RECOVERING OUR SPIRITUAL FOCUS
(Heb. 12:1-2)

I like television. Most nights when we are home, Linda and I watch television after dinner. We start with the evening news, then we watch whatever suits our fancy—sports programming, reality shows, sitcoms, dramas, movies, you name it. As much as I like watching television, however, my life would be pretty shallow if that's all I did.

Television is a poor substitute for reality because television presents a narrow, distorted view of the world. For one thing, most of the people on television are young, affluent, and physically attractive. Even those who are not young look better than most people their age. Minorities, older people, poor people, those with disabilities, and those who are ordinary-looking are vastly under-represented on television. For another thing, the morality on television, especially when it comes to violence and sexual mores, is grossly distorted. But I suppose my biggest concern about the programming on television is that most of it lacks a spiritual focus. Religion is seldom mentioned on network television, and when it is portrayed, it is often in a negative light.

So, if we want to recover a spiritual focus to life, we'll have to look elsewhere than television. If we want to recover a spiritual focus, we can look to nature, and to relationships, and to the depths of our own spiritual being.

First, we can recover our spiritual focus by looking to nature. In his book *The Re-Enchantment of Everyday Life*, Thomas Moore noted that human life began in a garden, Eden, and that ultimately, we will return to a garden, Paradise. The two images of the Garden of Eden and the Garden of Paradise give good reason, Moore said, for spending time in gardens and in the beauty of nature to get back in touch with the spiritual side of life. Perhaps you remember that verse from a poem by Dorothy Frances Gurney:

The kiss of the sun for pardon,
The song of the birds for mirth,
One is nearer God's Heart in a garden
Than anywhere else on earth.

During a vacation to British Columbia, Canada, Linda and I visited the world-famous Butchart Gardens, just north of Victoria on Vancouver Island. I'm not much of a connoisseur when it comes to flowers—I hardly know a pansy from a petunia—but I was enthralled by the Butchart Gardens.

A maze of gardens, paths, ponds, and lawns, Butchart Gardens covers more than 50 acres. It is really a series of gardens, each with its own theme—a Sunken Garden, a Japanese Garden, an Italian Garden, a Rose Garden, and more. From March through October, the Gardens offer a continuous display of spectacular scenery, with flowers in bloom without interruption. To accomplish that feat, a million-plus bedding plants are used, representing at least 700 varieties of flowers, grasses, and shrubs. It is the most gorgeous display of nature that you could imagine.

We spent an entire morning wandering along the paths, stopping to see and to smell the exquisite flowers and other natural surroundings. Butchart Gardens is a beautiful place, a tranquil place, a spiritual place. More than a million visitors a year find their way there, and if we ever get back to Vancouver Island, we will find our way there again.

Nature can put us in touch with the spiritual side of life. The Psalmist wrote, "The heavens are telling the glory of God and the firmament proclaims his handiwork" (Ps. 19:1). The glory of God is revealed in the natural world. Getting back to nature, whether it's a garden or a forest or a field or a mountain or a lake or a river or the seashore, can kindle within us a renewed awareness of God's presence in our world and in our lives. That's one of the reasons I like to play golf—it gets me outside into the world of nature, amid the trees and grasses and flowers of earth. Many of us spend far too much time inside, and it is easy to have our senses dulled to God's presence when we are cut off from the natural world. The poet William Wordsworth wrote:

> The world is too much with us; late and soon,
> Getting and spending, we lay waste our powers;
> Little we see in nature that is ours.

One way to get back in touch with God is to get back in touch with the natural world he created.

A second way to recover our spiritual focus is to spend more time with God's people, the church. God is revealed in the beauties of nature, but God is also revealed in the lives of people who are dedicated to him. Nature can reveal the presence of God, but not everyone sees God in nature. One person can look at the sky or the world around us and give God glory and praise. Another person can look at the same sky and natural world and say, "I don't see a thing." That is because God does not force himself upon us. God is there, but we must have faith to see. And the way that most of us develop that faith is through our contact with other Christians.

It was as a child, in the home of my parents and in the home of my grandparents, that I first learned about God. It was also as a child going to Sunday School that teachers taught me about God. As I grew, many other Christians had powerful and positive influences on my life. Music leaders, youth leaders, pastors, and other Christian young people helped me to develop my spiritual sensitivity and awareness of God's presence. If all I had to go on were nature, I don't know that I would have ever found God in my life. But I had more than nature. I had the fellowship of the church. I had other Christians who taught me, mentored me, and encouraged me in my spiritual journey. And somewhere along the way I found God—or should I say, God found me. It still happens that way.

We get in touch with God through the lives of people in the church. We recover our spiritual focus by spending time with other people who love God and seek to serve him. That is why involvement in the life of the church is so important. You may find God at work, especially if there are other Christians in the workplace. You may find God at school, especially if there are believers there. You may find God at home, especially if other members of your family are committed to Jesus Christ. But the place where you are most likely to find God is in the church, where people come together for the purpose of worshipping God and making him known. Show me a person who has lost his or her spiritual focus, and I'll show you a person who probably has lost touch with the church. But show me a person who is on fire for God, and I'll show you a person who is deeply committed to God's people.

A third way—the most important way—to recover our spiritual focus is to take that journey inward to the heart of our souls, where we can meet Jesus Christ. Here I'm talking about meeting God in prayer, Bible study, worship, and personal commitment to Jesus Christ. Hebrews says that the best way to recover our spiritual focus is to look to Jesus, to keep the eyes of our souls fixed on him. Hebrews calls Jesus the "pioneer and perfecter" of our faith.

Jesus is the pioneer of our faith because, through his death on the cross, he opened the way for all of us to come to God. A pioneer is one who goes ahead and blazes the trail for others to follow. That is what Jesus has done: he blazed a trail of faith through his absolute obedience to God, an obedience that led him to die on the cross. Not only is Jesus the pioneer of our faith, but Jesus is also the perfecter of our faith.

Jesus is the one who makes our faith perfect and complete. Nature can point us to God, but the pathway of nature leads to an incomplete, imperfect faith. Other people can point us to God, but that pathway is incomplete and imperfect too. Only Jesus is the perfecter of our faith. When we trust in and follow Jesus, our faith in God is made complete and perfect.

I mentioned our visit to Butchart Gardens, but how and why those gardens were created is a story in itself. The year was 1904, and the 130-acre property on which Butchart Gardens is now located was a wasteland. It was an abandoned limestone quarry, barren and desolate, an ugly scar left upon the earth. This was before environmental laws forced companies to reclaim strip mining sites. But the wife of the owner, Jenny Butchart, had a vision for this forsaken landscape. She wanted to restore the soul to the property by converting it into a garden. That was no easy feat. To transform that rocky pit into a sunken garden required tons of topsoil. Jenny Butchart requisitioned rich dirt from nearby farmland and had it transported to the site by horse-drawn carts. Her husband was so pleased with the reclamation project that he encouraged Jenny to create other gardens. First, she added a Japanese garden, then later an Italian garden, then later a rose garden. Gradually, the barren wasteland was transformed back to a state of natural beauty, and its spiritual focus was restored.

Our lives can become like a desolate landscape when we lose our spiritual focus. But God wants to do a reclamation project on each of us if we will let him. When we allow Jesus to come into our hearts, when we maintain a vital relationship with him, a transformation begins to take place. Looking to Jesus can turn the barren pits of our hearts into a garden of God's grace.

A CLOUD OF WITNESSES
(Heb. 12:1-2)

My friend Ron Knode was a runner. He was on the track-and-field team at the United States Naval Academy. His teammates knew him as a fierce competitor at any distance. His roommate said that Ron would wake well before reveille and run five miles. In an early spring track meet against the University of Maryland in 1965, an Academy teammate had a lock on first place in the half-mile race. He was coming around the final turn and into the homestretch when Ron bolted past him and broke the tape. The teammate was disappointed that Ron had beaten him, but he was gratified that they both had beaten the hotshot half-miler from Maryland who had been the New York state interscholastic champion. Years later Ron was the voice of Navy track-and-field and cross-country meets. He entertained spectators in the stands and competitors on the field with his humorous asides. Even though he was no longer running competitively, Ron still wanted to be involved in the races.

Our scripture compares the Christian life to a race. The author of the book of Hebrews wrote, "let us run with perseverance the race that is set before us." Living a faithful Christian life is not easy. It requires stamina, perseverance, and consistent effort. But we do not run the race of faith alone. We have fellow believers who encourage us as we run together. That is why it is important to attend church. There is camaraderie from being with other Christians who are also trying to follow Jesus. Plus, we have the examples of those who have gone before us and finished the race and kept the faith, as Paul put it in 2 Timothy.

In Hebrews, the author pictures those who have run the race before us as a great cloud of witnesses, gathered above the field of competition, cheering us along as we press toward the finish line. Hebrews 11 mentions many heroes of the faith in the Old Testament as members of that great cloud of witnesses. They are our spiritual ancestors, too, but we also have modern-day witnesses who have gone before us and finished the race.

Ron Knode died on May 31, 2012 at the age of 66. His passing was a tremendous shock and loss to all who knew him. He was so active, so vital, so full of life. It was hard to go on without him, especially at the early worship service at Village Baptist Church where he led the music, and in the choir, and in so many other aspects of our church's life. His family and his friends miss him more than we can say. But as much as we miss Ron Knode, we are grateful for the kind of person he was.

Ron lived out his faith throughout his life. His roommate at the Naval Academy said this about Ron: "He was the only one I knew that could have a good time drinking a root beer in the Steerage under the rotunda. I admired him deep down, because he was dedicated to his religion and lived by its principles." Another classmate said, "Beyond being the smartest and the sharpest guy in our ranks, he was of unrelenting good humor and true to his principles throughout his life."

That's why we count Ron Knode among that great cloud of witnesses who has run the race before us and is now looking down and cheering us on. There's one more story I'd like to tell you about Ron that exemplifies his character. It was reported in the Naval Academy alumni magazine by his teammate Dave Wallace.

Dave remembers the 1967 cross-country race against Army, certainly one of the most important races of the year. The five-mile, cross-country course took runners across the Severn River at the Naval Station and wound through the woods until the final half-mile uphill stretch to the finish line. In that race Ron was the first to cross the road, with a 20-yard lead over his teammate Dave. Ron was sure to be the winner with the finish line in sight.

But as Ron looked back to see how close his competitors were, he saw no Army runners. There was Dave 20 yards behind, so Ron slowed up to allow Dave to come up alongside him. Ron was willing to sacrifice his solo victory over Army to allow his teammate to win the race with him. Then, Ron and Dave looked back, and they saw their teammate Jim Dare another 20 yards back, and even further back their teammate Chip Foulsham. Ron and Dave slowed up so that Jim and Chip could join them. Finally, the four Navy runners crossed the finish line arm-in-arm, sharing together the victory that Ron could have claimed for himself. Dave said it was the most selfless act he had ever seen in sports. But that's who Ron Knode was. He lived his Christian life through and through.

We remember those who have gone before, and who are looking down and cheering us on as we run with perseverance the race that is set before us. Ron Knode joined that cloud of witnesses who ran with perseverance the race that was set before them. They left for us a legacy of faithful devotion to Christ and his church. How grateful we are to have been inspired by their examples of faithful Christian living. But our greatest inspiration comes from Jesus himself, the pioneer and perfecter of our faith. "For the sake of the joy that was set before him [he] endured the cross, disregarded its shame, and has taken his seat at the right hand of the throne of God." That's the finish line, the goal that is set before us, the joy of finishing the race and keeping the faith.

Jesus never promised that living the Christian life would be easy. But he did promise to be with us always. Only by living for Jesus will we find the joy of our salvation. Only by following him will we finally cross the finish line and make it all the way home.

QUESTIONS FOR DISCUSSION REFLECTION

1. Who is among your great "cloud of witnesses"?
2. What weights do you need to lay aside to run the race?
3. How can we look to Jesus?
4. How can you allow Jesus to perfect your faith?
5. What is the goal toward which you run?

CHAPTER 5

Let Mutual Love Continue
(Hebrews 13:1-5)

Let mutual love continue. Do not neglect to show hospitality to strangers... Remember those who are in prison...; those who are being tortured... Let marriage be held in honor by all, and let the marriage bed be kept undefiled... Keep your lives free from the love of money, and be content with what you have...."

(Heb. 13:1-5 NRSV)

These concluding admonitions in Hebrews 13 read as a summary of Christian ethical behaviors and attitudes. The undergirding principle is mutual love. The reference to entertaining angels without knowing it is an allusion to Genesis 18:1-8, when Abraham welcomed three visitors, thus showing hospitality to strangers. Remembering those in prison and those who are being tortured is an echo of Jesus' parable of the Great Judgment in Matthew 25:35-46, in which our standing before God when the Son of Man comes is directly related to how we have treated "the least of these." Fidelity in marriage and the renunciation of avarice are also characteristics of the Christian life. We are to be content with what we have, because above all, we have the promise of God's presence in our lives. As the Lord said to Joshua, "I will be with you; I will not fail you or forsake you" (Josh. 1:5).

SACRIFICES PLEASING TO GOD
(Heb. 13:1-5, 16)

My grandmother was not a wealthy woman. Her husband, my grandfather Bruce Shulkey, for whom I was named, was a schoolteacher, and then a school administrator. He died before he reached retirement age. My grandmother spent the last 26 years of her life as a widow, living a simple life on a relatively modest income. The only car she owned after my grandfather died was the one that my family had given her in 1963. She lived in the same two-bedroom house for most of her adult life. Yet, despite her limited financial means, my grandmother was an incredibly generous woman.

She was diligent about giving her tithe to the church, even when she could no longer attend. When I was in college, every letter she sent me would have a five- or ten-dollar bill neatly folded inside. Sometimes she would write a note suggesting I use the money to get a haircut; but most of the time there were no strings attached.

Late in life, my grandmother received an unexpected royalty payment from some mineral rights to a long-forgotten oil well in west Texas. It was only a few hundred dollars, but instead of keeping it for herself, she divided the royalty payment among her three grandchildren. She did not think of it as a sacrifice, but we knew it was. Her whole life was a sacrifice of love. That's not surprising because my grandmother was a deeply committed Christian. And in its purest expression, the Christian life is a sacrifice of love.

The concept of sacrifice is practiced in many religions. Offering a sacrifice to God was a central part of the Jewish religion. Worship centered around bringing a sacrificial offering to the Temple and laying it on the altar as an act of dedication and repentance. The sacrificial offering might be a food, or a drink, or even a live animal. Whatever it was, it would be something of value, and something given to God as an act of worship. The Jews believed that if they offered their sacrifices with sincerity, God would accept their gifts and forgive their sins. That is the background to the book of Hebrews, which uses the Jewish ritual of sacrifice to explain the death of Christ and the obligations of the Christian life.

According to Hebrews, the death of Jesus on the cross was the ultimate sacrificial offering for sin, a sacrifice that God offered on our behalf. Because Jesus died for our sins, it is no longer necessary to bring food or drink or animals and lay them on the altar as a sacrifice. Indeed, in most churches, the altar is the Communion table, and the bread and the cup represent the sacrifice that God made through the death of Jesus on the cross. That is why the ritual of sacrifice is no longer a central part of worship for Christians.

But in a deeper sense, sacrifice is still central to the Christian life. The sacrifices that God wants from us are not offerings of food or drink or animals, but lives dedicated to him. In Hebrews 13 we read some of the qualities of lives that are dedicated to God.

Mutual, or brotherly, love: The author of Hebrews wrote, "let brotherly love continue." The Greek word for this type of love is *philadelphia*, from which the city in Pennsylvania got its name. Love for each other is an essential quality of the Christian life. Brotherly or sisterly love is more than an emotion; it is something we do. It begins with an attitude of respect for other Christians and a genuine concern for their well-being. It goes on to include kind words and generous actions. Loving other Christians is a sacrifice each of us is called to make.

Hospitality to strangers: In the ancient world, traveling was dangerous. Most inns were filthy, infested with fleas, lice, and other vermin. They were also expensive, unsafe, and of low moral repute. In many places, inns were little more than brothels. You can understand how a traveling Christian would not want to stay in such a place. So, Christians would be called upon to host other Christians in their homes, even persons they did not previously know. Today, most of us would be reluctant to invite someone we did not know to stay in our homes, because we are very security-conscious. We know better than to pick up hitchhikers or to open our homes to strangers. But hospitality is still an essential quality of the Christian life. At the very least, we try to make strangers feel welcome at church. And there may be occasions when we can invite Christians whom we do not know into our homes.

Sympathy for those in legal trouble: Most Christians today take pride in being law-abiding citizens. My guess is that most Christians have never been in jail, not even to visit. But many of the early Christians were arrested and thrown into prison. And

Christians today in other parts of the world are imprisoned for their beliefs. The early Christians would care for their fellow believers who were in prison by visiting them, taking them food, and sometimes even raising money for their release. Identifying with those who had been arrested was risky. But Christians saw it as a larger part of their mission to stand in solidarity with those who were suffering. Remembering those who are in prison is a sacrifice pleasing to God.

Fidelity in marriage: In a time in which adultery is common, we must recover the sanctity of marriage. We must honor marriage vows and resist temptations to unfaithfulness. That's an important reminder in a time when half of all marriages do not last. That's the bad news. But the good news is that half of all marriages grow stronger and better, especially when couples see their marriage as a part of their commitment to Christ.

Contentment with what we have: As Paul wrote, "the love of money is the root of all kinds of evil" (1 Tim. 6:10). In our society, perhaps the only temptation greater than sexual immorality is greed. We are bombarded with so many materialistic messages that we begin to imagine that money is the key to contentment. The truth is that most of us could be and should be content with what we have.

Generosity toward others: There are many genuinely needy people in the world, and we can do something to help their situation. Hebrews 13:16 directs, "Do not neglect to do good and to share what you have, for such sacrifices are pleasing to God." Village Baptist Church had an annual emphasis on world hunger, with a special offering designated for people in need. We also had regular offerings for the community food pantry, and we made sandwiches for a feeding program for impoverished neighborhoods. Jesus said that what we do for the least of his people, we do for him.

These sacrifices are pleasing to God: mutual love, hospitality to strangers, sympathy for prisoners, faithfulness in marriage, contentment, and generosity. I learned from my grandmother, and she learned from a lifetime of devotion to Christ, that the true measure of a life is not how much you have but how much you give.

HOSPITALITY TO STRANGERS
(Heb. 13:1-2, 16)

Some years ago, to celebrate our 25th wedding anniversary, Linda and I took a vacation trip to Hawaii. We had been accruing airline points on our credit card since our son Marc was in college, and we finally had enough for two free roundtrip tickets to Hawaii. At the time Robin and Janice, two former members of our church, were stationed on Oahu, just outside Honolulu, and they invited us to stay in their home while we were there. Robin met us at the airport after our long flight and welcomed us with fresh-flower leis that he placed around our necks. He chauffeured us to their beautiful lakefront home on the northeast side of the island in the town of Kailua. Janice and their son Griffin were there, along with their two dogs, Izzy and Sheba. For the next several days, they showed us all around the island.

We played golf at several military courses, including the spectacular seaside course at Kaneohe Bay Marine Corps base. Our hosts also took us to the famous north shore to watch the surfers, visit a Dole pineapple orchard, and tour the *Arizona Memorial* and the *U.S.S Arizona* battleship at Pearl Harbor. We ate dinner at some fantastic restaurants and also ate some wonderful meals that Robin and Janice prepared at their home. In short, we were treated royally. Robin and Janice put their lives on hold so they could devote their full attention to hosting us. Their hospitality was warm and gracious and generous, and we had a fantastic time being with them.

That was one of the benefits of being a pastor: we developed many wonderful friendships over the years, relationships that endure even after people move away. It is part of the *philadelphia*, the brotherly and sisterly love that the church is all about.

In Hebrews 13 the author wrote, "let *philadelphia* continue." (He wasn't predicting a victory for the Eagles in the Super Bowl or for the Phillies in the World Series!) *Philadelphia* was a Greek word—after which the city in Pennsylvania got its name—derived from two other Greek words: *philia*, meaning love, and *adelphos*, meaning brother. Put the two words together and we have brotherly love, or sisterly love, or mutual love. That is the kind of love we find, or should find, in the church.

One of the main missions of the church, one of the primary purposes of the fellowship of faith, is to let *philadelphia* continue. Time and again the Scriptures tell us that we are to love one another as Christ loves us. The way that we love one another is by treating each other with kindness, consideration, and respect. But as important as *philadelphia* is, that is not the only purpose of the church. Brotherly/sisterly love is vital, but are called to love more than those who are in the fellowship of the church. We are called to love outsiders too.

Hebrews 13:2 instructs, "Do not neglect to show hospitality to strangers, for by doing that some have entertained angels without knowing it." There is another Greek word that we should place alongside *philadelphia*. It's the word *philozenias*, translated into English as "show hospitality" or "entertain." The text reads, "do not neglect *philozenias*." In other words, do not neglect to show hospitality to strangers; do not neglect to entertain outsiders. The Greek *philozenias* is also a compound of two other Greeks words, the same word for love, and the word *xenos*, which means stranger or alien or outsider. So, *philozenias* literally means "love for strangers." It is commonly translated "hospitality to strangers."

The Greek word for hospitality has an English derivative, xenophile. A xenophile is someone who loves or is attracted to foreigners or aliens or strangers. In contract, a xenophobe is someone who hates or fears foreigners or aliens or strangers. There are probably more xenophobes than xenophiles, more people who fear strangers than people who love strangers. It is a common human tendency to be fearful or suspicious or wary of people who are different from the way we are. People of different races or cultures or social classes tend to be segregated from one another in most societies. But it doesn't have to be that way. Children who are raised in a multiracial, multicultural, multi-socioeconomic environment are less likely to be xenophobes and more likely to be xenophiles. They are less likely to fear strangers and more likely to love strangers. And the church should be at the vanguard of *philozenias*, breaking down those barriers of race and culture and social class. As Paul said in Galatians 3:28, "There is no longer Jew or Greek, there is no longer slave or free, there is no longer male and female; for all of you are one in Christ Jesus." So, the church has a second mission in addition to *philadelphia*: mutual love. Our second purpose is *philozenias*—love for outsiders, hospitality to strangers.

Perhaps you remember the story from Genesis 18. Abraham and his wife Sarah had set up their tent beside the oaks of Mamre. In the heat of the day, Abraham looked up and saw three men standing outside the tent. Abraham rushed to meet them and welcome them. He brought water to wash their feet and bread to satisfy their hunger. Then he invited the three strangers to stay for a while and refresh themselves. Sarah baked cakes, and Abraham selected a calf from his herd to be slaughtered and prepared for a meal. Abraham sat with the three strangers under the oak tree outside the tent and ate.

After they had eaten, one of the three asked Abraham, "Where is your wife?" Abraham replied, "There, in the tent." One of the three said, "I will return to you in due season, and your wife Sarah shall have a son." Sarah was listening on the other side of the entrance to the tent. She and Abraham were both advanced in years, and Sarah was well beyond childbearing capability. So, Sarah laughed at the idea that she would bear a son. But the stranger said, "Is anything too wonderful for the Lord? At the set time I will return to you, in due season, and Sarah shall have a son."

Abraham and Sarah had entertained angels without knowing it. When the strangers first appeared in the noonday sun, Abraham had not recognized them as being from God. But he welcomed them and showed hospitality to them. Only later did it become clear that the three strangers represented the Lord himself. Remembering this incident in the life of Abraham and Sarah, the writer of Hebrews wrote, "Do not neglect to show hospitality to strangers, for by doing that some have entertained angels without knowing it."

For one week every winter, my church showed hospitality to strangers. As many as 25–30 homeless guests would arrive at our church building around 7:00 p.m., transported by county-operated vans. We would have a meal ready for them, with tables set up in the fellowship hall, along with beds for sleeping. The next morning, we would serve them breakfast and provide bag lunches to take for later. The homeless guests would return every night for a week. Volunteers from neighboring churches would help in providing the food. Volunteers from our church would stay every night, serve meals, do laundry, interact with the guests, and help in other ways. All of this was a part of our *philozenias*, our hospitality to strangers. Who knows? Maybe we were entertaining angels without knowing it.

In a sense, we are all guests in God's house. The Lord's Supper reminds us of that. Jesus is the host, and he prepared the supper with his sacrifice on the cross. Jesus invites us to share from his table, not as strangers, but as sisters and brothers he loves.

THE GRASS IS ALWAYS GREENER
(Heb. 13:1-5)

If you could live anywhere in America, where would you most like to live? That was the question posed some years ago by the Pew Research Center to a sampling of Americans. Out of a listing of 30 major metropolitan areas, the city voted most popular was Denver, Colorado: 43 percent of those surveyed said they would like to live in Denver (or its surrounding metropolitan area). I was surprised. I figured the most popular city would be San Diego. In fact, that was number two: 40 percent said they would like to live in San

Diego. The third most popular city was Seattle. Numbers four and five were in Florida: Orlando and Tampa. The lowest ranking cities were Cincinnati, Cleveland, and at the very bottom, Detroit. Only 8 percent of those surveyed said they would want to live in Detroit.

Now wait a minute, you might say, some of those low-ranking cities are nice places. I agree. I suspect the popularity of some of those higher ranked cities is due to good publicity more than any objective criteria. But here's the thing: a lot of people are restless. Of those surveyed, 46 percent said they would rather live in a different community than where they were living when the survey was taken.

In Hebrews 13 the writer says, "Be content with what you have." Be content—that is easier said than done. I am reminded about the little old lady whose eyesight was failing. She had three sons, and each son wanted to give his mother something in her twilight years to make her life happier.

The first son gave his mother a new house. It was a mansion, 15 rooms, with all the modern conveniences. The lady said to him: "Son, I want to thank you for your most thoughtful gift. It is a gorgeous house. In fact, it is too good for me. It is far more than I need. I live in just a few rooms now, and I don't need the responsibility of taking care of a place like that. So, please, keep the house, but thank you anyway."

The second son gave his mother a new car. It was big, fancy, and far better than any car she had ever owned. The lady said to him: "Son, I want to thank you for your most thoughtful gift. It is a gorgeous car. In fact, it is too good for me. It is far more than I need. As you know, my eyesight is not what it used to be, so I don't drive very much anymore, just to the hair salon and the grocery store and to church. I really don't need a car like that. So, please keep the car, but thank you anyway."

The third son, seeing how his brothers had failed to give their mother what she wanted, came up with a most unusual gift. He gave his mother a parrot. But it was not just an ordinary parrot. This son had spent months and months training the parrot to memorize passages from the Bible. The lady said to him: "Son, I want to thank you for your most thoughtful gift. That chicken was delicious!"

Hebrews instructs us to "be content with what you have." The question is: How? In a book titled *The How of Happiness*, a psychology professor at the University of California, Riverside, argues that 40 percent of our happiness is within our control. She says that 50 percent of our happiness is determined by our genetics, by the personalities we inherited from our parents, that influence our basic disposition. The remaining 10 percent of happiness is determined by circumstances, such as an illness or a divorce or a death, on the negative side, or by a birth or a marriage or a financial windfall, on the positive side. But even with 50 percent of our contentment determined by our genes, and 10 percent determined by our circumstances, the remaining 40 percent of our contentment comes from what we can do to positively improve our outlook on life.

What is the secret to tapping into that 40 percent of contentment that is within our control? Hebrews 13 provides some clues.

"Let mutual love continue" (v. 1): The Greek word is *philadelphia*, which means "brotherly love." One factor in contentment is brotherly love or "mutual love." In other

words, if you want to be content, focus on personal relationships. People who have positive, loving relationships with family and friends are more content than people who are socially isolated. That is one big advantage of being part of a church. Within the Christian community, we are not alone. As the old hymn goes, "Blest be the tie that binds our hearts in Christian love. Our fears, our hopes, our aims are one, our comforts and our cares." If you want to be content, focus on personal relationships.

"Do not neglect to show hospitality to strangers… remember those who are in prison" (vv. 2-3): If you want to be content, do something for someone else. People who get outside of themselves and help others are more content than those who focus only on themselves. Study after study has shown that people who volunteer and lend a hand to help someone else feel better about themselves and are more content with their lives. A study published in the Journal of Urban Health tracked a group of senior adults in Baltimore who helped in public elementary schools. The study found that those who volunteered scored higher in physical and cognitive abilities than those who did not participate. If you want to be content, focus on doing something for someone else.[1]

"Let marriage be held in honor by all" (v. 4): If you want to be content, focus on your marriage and your family. People who are happy in their marriage and family life are content people. Of course, family life is not just for those who are married. Single people can also be a part of extended families. But marriage is the basic unit of family life, and faithful marriage contributes to contentment. Conversely, Hebrews says that "God will judge fornicators and adulterers."

"Keep your lives free from the love of money" (v. 5): In other words, if you want to be content, don't focus on money. Of course, some amount of money is necessary, but there are a lot of things in life more important than money. Our culture gives us the opposite message, telling us that the secret to happiness is money and the things that money can buy. Sooner or later, many of the things that money can buy end up at a yard sale or on a junk heap. Money can buy temporary pleasures, but money cannot buy lasting happiness. If you want to be content, don't focus on money.

"I will never leave you or forsake you" (Heb. 13:5): In other words, if you want to be content, focus on Jesus. He is the source of lasting happiness and true contentment. When all else fails, when all else passes away, Jesus will be there for us. He will never leave us or forsake us.

A lot of people think the grass is greener in Denver or San Diego or someplace else. But the Bible tells us to be content with what you have right now. And you can be content if you will focus on personal relationships, helping others, and your marriage and family instead of focusing on money, and above all, focus on Jesus. Most of us already have what we need to be happy. Sure, there will be circumstances that change our mood—that is 10 percent of our contentment. Yes, we inherited a basic disposition that affects our outlook on life. That is 50 percent. But at least 40 percent of our contentment is under our control. It is a matter of attitude, priorities, and faith.

QUESTIONS FOR DISCUSSION/REFLECTION

1. How can you let mutual love continue?
2. How can you show hospitality to strangers?
3. What persons in need can you remember and help?
4. What can you do to hold marriage in honor, whether you are married or not?
5. How can you be content with what you have?

NOTE

[1] Cited in *AARP the Magazine*, November/December 2008.

CHAPTER 6

FAITH AND DEEDS
(James 2:14-17)

What good is it, my brothers and sisters, if someone claims to have faith but has no deeds? Can such faith save them? Suppose a brother or a sister is without clothes and daily food. If one of you says to them, "Go in peace; keep warm and well fed," but does nothing about their physical needs, what good is it? In the same way, faith by itself, if it is not accompanied by action, is dead.

(Jas. 2:14-17 NIV)

Faith without works is dead. In James 2:8, the author describes the verse that Jesus quoted from Leviticus 19:18, "You shall love your neighbor as yourself," as the "royal law." Jesus called it the second greatest commandment. Love for others is expressed in actions on their behalf.

James was especially concerned with the disparities between the rich and the poor. At the beginning of James 2, he decries acts of favoritism toward the rich and against the poor. He imagines a rich person being warmly welcomed into the Christian assembly, while a poor person is being relegated to a lesser place. James says that "believers in our glorious Lord Jesus Christ must not show favoritism" (v.1). Rather, believers should be concerned for the poor, and translate their concern into deeds. Faith is expressed not just by what we say, but even more by what we do.

LIVING FAITH
(Jas. 2:8-17)

The book of James is different from every other one in the New Testament. Although it begins as a letter, most of it reads like a collection of wise sayings. James is a kind of "user's manual" for what it means to be a Christian. But that is not as simple as it sounds. If someone identifies herself or himself as a Christian, you cannot be sure exactly what that means.

For some people, being a Christian means they live in a country where Christianity is the majority religion. For them, being a Christian is almost akin to being an American. There is even a term for it: Christian nationalism.

For others, being a Christian means their family has a Christian identity. Maybe their parents or grandparents identified themselves as Christians. So, for them, being a Christian is a matter of being related to someone who is or was a Christian.

For some, being a Christian means they are members of a church. Maybe they were baptized as infants, and even if they have no current church relationship, they still consider themselves affiliated with a church, and therefore a Christian.

For others, being a Christian means believing in Christ. Of course, what it means to believe in Christ can have a wide variety of interpretations.

For some, being a Christian means they have accepted Jesus as their Savior, which presupposes having made a faith commitment at one time, although it does not necessarily presuppose a particular lifestyle.

For some, being a Christian means ascribing to a certain set of beliefs. It is more propositional than anything else.

And yet for others, being a Christian is primarily a matter of how you act. For them, a Christian has a certain lifestyle: a Christian does or does not do certain things.

A friend's daughter was scheduled to graduate from Taylor University in Upland, Indiana. I went to the school's web site to find out more about it. Taylor University identifies itself as a Christian school, "an interdenominational liberal arts university of evangelical faith." What does it mean for a college to identify itself as "Christian"?

For Taylor University, it means that the administration, faculty, staff, and students are guided by certain principles. These principles are spelled out in a document called the "Life Together Covenant." To be a part of the Taylor University community, administrators, faculty, staff, and students are expected to act in a certain way. The covenant specifies certain "Prohibited Behaviors," for example:

> Certain behaviors are expressly prohibited in Scripture and therefore to be avoided by all members of the community. They include theft, lying, dishonesty, gossip, slander, backbiting, profanity, vulgarity, crude language, sexual immorality (including adultery, homosexual behavior, premarital sex, and involvement with pornography in any form), drunkenness, immodesty of dress, and occult practice.
>
> Social dancing is not permitted on or away from campus. However, acceptable forms of expression may include sanctioned folk dances, dances that are designed to worship God, dancing at weddings, and the use of choreography in drama, musical productions, and athletic events.

In addition, all members of the campus community are prohibited from using tobacco and alcohol and from gambling in any form.

From what I can tell, Taylor University is a fine school. I went to a Christian college myself, Baylor University, a Baptist school in Waco, Texas. When I was a student there in the 1970s, many of those same behaviors also were prohibited. I understand the need to specify behaviors that Christians should not do. But there is a danger in becoming so legalistic that being a Christian is reduced to a list of "don'ts": Don't drink, don't smoke, don't chew, and don't go with girls that do.

For James, being a Christian involves both what you believe and how you act. He specified certain prohibited behaviors. In James 2:11 he quoted two of the Ten Commandments, "You

Faith and Deeds

shall not commit adultery," and "You shall not murder." Clearly, adultery and murder are outside the parameters of Christian conduct. But James was not just concerned about what Christians should not do. He was also concerned about what Christians should do. In James 2:8 he wrote, "If you really keep the royal law found in Scripture, 'Love your neighbor as yourself,' you are doing right." That command to love your neighbor as yourself came from Jesus, who said it was among the greatest commandments, second only to loving God. James called it "the royal law."

So, being a Christian involves what you believe, but it also involves what you do and don't do. James said there are two parts to the Christian life: faith and deeds. Faith is what you believe; deeds are what you do. Faith is an attitude; deeds are actions. Both are necessary for Christian living. James said that unless we put our faith into action, it is meaningless and empty. Faith without action is dead. James gave some examples of putting faith into action. Suppose someone is hungry or in need of clothing. It is not enough to wish them well. No, we must do something to alleviate their suffering and meet their needs. Faith and action go hand in hand.

According to Professor David Blight, who teaches American history at Yale University, near the end of the American Civil War, the dead were everywhere. About 620,000 soldiers had been killed. That was a huge percentage of the population. If the same number of Americans per capita had died during the Vietnam War, there would be 4,000,000 names on the Vietnam Memorial instead of the almost 60,000 that are inscribed.

The once-beautiful port city of Charleston, South Carolina was particularly devastated by the fighting in the Civil War. The place where the war had begun was in ruins by the spring of 1865. After a long siege, prolonged bombardments, and numerous fires, the city was largely abandoned by its white residents. The majority of those who remained in Charleston were black residents, mostly former slaves, along with a few white missionaries and teachers.

The last year of the war the Confederates had converted a plantation horse track, once used by southern gentry for races, into an outdoor prison for captured Union soldiers. The conditions of the prison in the interior of the racetrack were atrocious. At least 257 Union prisoners of war died of exposure or disease. Their bodies were hastily buried in a mass grave behind the grandstand before the Confederate prison guards retreated ahead of the advancing Union forces. Among the first Union troops to enter Charleston in the spring of 1865 was the 21st United States Colored Infantry Regiment. They marched up Meeting Street singing songs of liberation.

After the formal surrender of the city, some 28 black freedmen went to the site of the mass grave behind the prison camp. Grateful for the sacrifices that had been made, the freedmen exhumed the bodies of the Union soldiers and reinterred each one in an individual grave. The freedmen also built a fence around the graveyard and declared it a Union cemetery. They whitewashed the fence and built an archway over the entrance on which they inscribed, "Martyrs of the Race Course."

On May 1, 1865, a crowd of up to 10,000 mainly black residents of Charleston processed to the graveyard to pay their respects. The procession began with 3,000 black schoolchildren carrying armloads of roses and singing. Hundreds of black women followed with baskets of flowers, wreaths, and crosses to decorate the graves. Then the black men followed, marching in cadence, followed by contingents of Union soldiers and other black and white citizens.

There were sermons, singing, and readings from scripture. Finally, there was a picnic on the grounds as the participants listened to speeches and watched the soldiers drill. It was an event to honor the dead and to celebrate the freedom that their sacrifice had won. Those freedmen and their fellow citizens put their faith into action.[1]

The old racetrack is still there, not too far from the Citadel. The oval roadway is in Hampton Park, and the military cadets often jog on the track, perhaps unaware of its history. The old cemetery is long gone. The Union soldiers who had been buried there by the freedmen as "Martyrs of the Race Course," were reinterred yet again in the 1880s and moved to a national cemetery some miles away. But thanks to Professor Blight, the memory of what happened there on a day in May in 1865 has been reclaimed.

Faith is not just what we believe; faith is what we do. Faith without deeds is dead. But when we put our beliefs into action, ours is a living faith. May we who have been freed by the ultimate sacrifice that Jesus made put our faith into action. And may we demonstrate our love for God by fulfilling the royal law to love our neighbors as we love ourselves.

IF JESUS IS LORD
(Jas. 2:1-17)

Biblical scholars believe that the earliest confession of faith among the first Christians was the simple affirmation, "Jesus is Lord." As you read the New Testament, Jesus is described as Lord perhaps more than any other way. His first disciples called Jesus "Lord." In his many letters to the churches, Paul invariably referred to our Lord Jesus Christ. Certainly, Jesus was known by many other titles.

Jesus referred to himself as the Son of Man, or the Human One, as the Common English Bible translates it. He became known as the Son of God. He was called Master, Teacher, Rabbi. Ultimately, he became known as the Savior, the Messiah, the Christ. In fact, Messiah or Christ became his second name in Christian thinking and writing. (Christ was the Greek name for the Jewish name Messiah.) But beyond all those titles, the most universal confession of faith among the early Christians was the simple affirmation, "Jesus is Lord."

What exactly does it mean to affirm that "Jesus is Lord"? Saying that Jesus is Lord means that Jesus has authority in and over our lives. Every decision we make, every action we take, every word we speak, every thought we think occurs under the authority of our Lord Jesus Christ—at least, that is the goal. If Jesus is Lord of our lives, we will live differently than we would if he were not Lord, including in the way we treat other people. If Jesus were not Lord, then we would be selfish and self-centered, concerned only about our own needs and wants and pleasures. We would live only for ourselves. But because Jesus is Lord, we cannot be concerned only about ourselves.

Jesus made it plain, both through his teachings and through his example, that we are to love other people just as much as we love ourselves. And the kind of love that

Jesus taught and demonstrated was not emotional sentimentality, but specific actions designed to enhance the well-being of other people.

If Jesus is Lord, we must be concerned about the poor, but not only concerned: we must do something to help them. James made the connection between Christian concern for the poor and concrete actions to help the poor. He said it is not enough simply to wish the poor well, but it is our responsibility to do something to help them. This was not something James dreamed up. Care for the poor is a major theme of the entire Bible.

The Law of Moses in the first five books of the Bible makes it clear that God's people are to care for the needs of the poor. Consider this example:

> When you reap the harvest of your land, you shall not reap to the very edges of your field, or gather the gleanings of your harvest; you shall leave them for the poor and for the alien: I am the Lord your God. (Lev. 23:22)

The prophets of the Old Testament had a lot to say about mercy and justice for the poor, for example:

> Let justice roll down like waters, and righteousness like an ever-flowing stream.
> (Amos 5:24)

> The Spirit of the Lord God is upon me because the Lord has anointed me; he has sent me to bring good news to the oppressed, to bind up the brokenhearted, to proclaim liberty to the captives, and release to the prisoners. (Isa. 61:1)

Even the Psalms and the Proverbs talk about caring for the poor, including among others:

> For the needy shall not be forgotten, nor the hope of the poor perish forever.
> (Ps. 9:18)

> Happy are those who consider the poor;
> the Lord delivers them in the day of trouble.
> (Ps. 41:1)

> Whoever is kind to the poor lends to the Lord, and will be repaid in full.
> (Prov. 19:17)

In the New Testament, Jesus told many parables about doing deeds of kindness and mercy: the parable of the good Samaritan, the parable of the sheep and the goats, and others. Paul made the collection for the poor in Jerusalem a major focus of his missionary travels as he went from church to church. And in the book of Acts, when Luke described the first church in Jerusalem in the earliest days of the Christian faith, he said there was not a needy person among them because they shared their goods in common. So, concern for the poor is not a peripheral issue in the Bible; it is central to what we are called to do as God's people. Jesus himself described his mission as preaching good news to the poor.

Every time a hungry child is fed, every time a sick person is ministered to, every time a person in need is given help, the forces of evil are pushed back and the kingdom of God is advanced. That is how we Christians can confront the evils of this world, by being doers of good. Edmund Burke, an 18th-century British statesman, said, "The only thing necessary for evil to triumph is for good men to do nothing." Evil will not triumph, because God is God, and God will inspire his people to do good in the world.

If Jesus is Lord, it will have an effect on the way we live. We will:

- …live redeemed, transformed lives.
- …be a part of the church.
- …give sacrificially of our incomes to support the Lord's work.
- …serve others in Christ's name.
- …make prayer a way of life.
- …live by the highest ethical standards.
- …treat others the way we want others to treat us.
- …love our neighbors as we love ourselves.
- …turn the other cheek, go the second mile, and forgive 70 times 7.
- …share our faith through our lifestyles and our words of witness and testimony.
- …work for peace and justice in the world.
- …feed the hungry, care for the needy, visit the sick, and minister to the hurting.
- …live in such a way that others see Jesus in us.

May God inspire us to be about his business and to put our faith into action, because Jesus is Lord.

FAITH WORKS
(Jas. 2:14-17)

Oftentimes people come to churches and ask for financial assistance. At my former church in Silver Spring, Maryland, it was several times a month. For some churches in downtown Washington, D.C., it might be several times a week. Poverty is a problem in our society. Millions of Americans live in poverty, and the rate is much higher for people of color than for whites. Many of those living in poverty are children.

In the county where my wife and I live, there are more homeless people on any given night than there are beds in shelters. That is why many houses of worship have banded together for the Warm Nights ministry in conjunction with the county social services department and a local nonprofit agency. During the cold winter months, houses of worship become temporary homeless shelters.

While poverty is a big problem in America, it is even more severe in many other countries. As Christians, we need to know about the needs around us: and, we have a responsibility to help. According to the Bible, helping others is not just an option—an assignment we can do to get extra credit. Helping others is an essential part of our identity as Christians. James makes it clear that faith without works is dead. It does not matter what we believe if those beliefs do not propel us into action. Good intentions are not enough. A benign sort of piety is not enough. James says, if we see someone in need and fail to do something to help, all our talk about faith is just so much hot air.

Most of us already know that. We consider ourselves to be compassionate and generous people. We are more than willing to do something to help those who are hurting. The problem is, we are not sure how. Maybe we need some practical suggestions for putting our faith into action, ideas for making compassion an ongoing part of our everyday lives.

Here is one suggestion: Every time you go to the grocery store, buy something extra for your community's and/or church's food pantry. Buy whatever is on special, if you like, to make your dollars go further. Buy food that provides the most "bang for the buck" nutrition-wise. Do this regularly. Every time you go to the store, add something to your list. At my church, we had a wooden box in the corner of the fellowship hall designated for the community food pantry. People could place their donations in the box and then members of the Missions Commission would deliver the contents to the pantry.

Here is another suggestion: Many of us come home with change or loose bills in our pockets or purses at the end of the day. Why not set aside loose change and/or bills for hunger relief? In the Old Testament the Jews had the law of gleanings to provide for widows and orphans. Farmers would leave some of their harvest behind as they were gathering their crops. Then the poor would go out into the fields and collect what was left. I see a parallel between the change and loose bills in our pockets and purses and the gleanings that were left in the fields. God expects us to give some of our excess to help people in need.

I have another suggestion: If you really want to help, work through existing relief agencies whenever possible. Unless you know someone on a personal basis, I would advise against giving money directly to an individual. Of course, if you know someone personally and you are familiar with their needs, a direct financial gift might be in order. But if you give money to someone whom you do not know, you may be doing more harm than good.

My church had a policy of not giving out money to people from outside our church who came seeking financial help. If someone were hungry, I would refer them to the community food pantry. Sometimes I would even go with them to a local fast-food restaurant and buy them a meal. We also kept a supply of gift cards to local fast-food outlets that I could give them. If someone were stranded and needed fuel for their vehicle to continue down the road, sometimes I would follow them to the gas station and provide fuel. If someone needed medicine, sometimes I would go with them to the local pharmacy and buy what I could for them. But I would not give money to people I did not know.

I heard about a lady in Texas who devised a practical way to help homeless people. She would prepare plastic bags with basic toiletries—soap, toothpaste, washcloth, and the like—and keep some of those bags in her car. If someone asked her for money, she would offer a bag. I know other people who keep a ready supply of fast-food gift certificates on hand. The point is, we want to help people who are in need without enabling any chemical dependency they might have. Although not everyone in poverty has an addiction, some homeless people do. Therefore, it is wise, whenever possible, to work through existing social service agencies.

Let's take it a step further. It is one thing to give a person something to eat, but it is even better to do something about the situation that made the person hungry in the first place. Here I am suggesting we allow our faith to inform our politics. As Christians, our concern for the poor should influence our political involvements. We can communicate with our elected officials about allocating our tax dollars to meet basic human needs. I realize public policy decisions are complex.

An insurance company sent me a packet of materials about the dangers of price controls. They wanted me to write a letter to our member of Congress to voice opposition to ceilings on health insurance premiums. A representative from the company called me to see if I had written the letter. I told him that I appreciated the information, but that I was still trying to figure out the ethical implications of price controls on health insurance. He laughed and told me that there was nothing in the Bible about health care reform. I replied, maybe not, but there is a lot in the Bible about compassion and justice.

If our religion does not influence our politics, our religion is not much good in the first place. Here is the test of good religion: Does it help people? Oliver Thomas, who served as general counsel for the Baptist Joint Committee for Religious Liberty, wrote in a column: "Christian religion is incarnational. If it doesn't feed you when you're hungry, clothe you when you're naked, visit you when you're sick, and hug you when you're lonely, God's not in it."[2]

The test of our faith is deeds of mercy and compassion. James does not say that doing good deeds will save us. He does not reduce religion to good works alone. To be sure, faith involves what we believe, the kind of relationship we have with God. But faith also involves what we do. James says that faith involves believing and doing. We are saved by our faith in Jesus Christ as our Savior and Lord, but we demonstrate our faith, live out our faith, by what we do.

John D. Rockefeller was born to a family of modest means on a farm in upstate New York in 1839. His father was a traveling salesman, and the family moved several times during his youth. His mother was a devoutly religious woman who taught John to work, to save, and to give. When the family moved to Strongsville, Ohio, John rented a room in the city so he could attend Central High School in Cleveland. He joined the Erie Street Baptist Church and became a trustee of the church at age 21.

At the age of 24, Rockefeller and a partner entered the oil business as refiners, just four years after the first oil well was drilled in western Pennsylvania. This was long before the invention of the automobile, but kerosene was being used for lighting. Recognizing the potential, Rockefeller organized the Standard Oil Company in 1870 at the age of

31. Twenty years later it was estimated that Standard Oil owned three-fourths of the petroleum business in the United States. Rockefeller retired from active leadership of the company in 1896, at the age of 57. He focused the rest of his life on philanthropy, on giving away the bulk of his fortune. Various Rockefeller foundations supported education, medical research, public health, scientific advancement, the arts, and Baptist and other Christian missionary organizations.

From his earliest years, when he had begun to earn money as a boy, Rockefeller had been giving away a share of his income to his church and other charities. He later wrote, "I believe it is every man's religious duty to get all he can honestly and to give all he can." Even before he became a rich man, Rockefeller made regular contributions to his church and to other causes. At the age of 21, not only was he giving to his own church in Cleveland, but he was also giving to a foreign Sunday School and to an African-American church. Support for religious institutions and African-American education remained two of his major philanthropic interests throughout his life. By the time he died in 1937, it is estimated that John D. Rockefeller had donated more than $540 million to charitable causes. Clearly, John D. Rockefeller put his faith into action.[3]

None of us is a John D. Rockefeller, but we can learn from the principles of his life. Rockefeller understood that we are not cisterns made for hoarding, but channels made for giving. He understood that every person has a mission, a calling, a religious duty, to give. He understood that faith is not only what you believe, but also what you do. We can make a difference. Our faith can make a difference in the lives of hurting people when we put our faith to work. God can use our hands, our hearts, our voices, and yes, our money. Jesus said that whatever we do for people in need, we do for him. We have faith. Now, what will we do?

QUESTIONS FOR DISCUSSION/REFLECTION

1. What is the relationship between faith and deeds?
2. Who are the needy in our midst?
3. What can we do to help them?
4. How can faith influence our political beliefs?
5. How much does God expect us to give?

NOTES

[1] http://www.davidwblight.com/memorial.html.
[2] *REPORT from the CAPITAL* (October 1993).
[3] Biographical information provided by Rockefeller Archive Center, revised September 1997.

CHAPTER 7

PRAY FOR EACH OTHER
(James 5:13-16)

> *If any of you are suffering, they should pray. If any of you are happy, they should sing. If any of you are sick, they should call for the elders of the church, and the elders should pray over them, anointing them with oil in the name of the Lord. Prayer that comes from faith will heal the sick, for the Lord will restore them to health. And if they have sinned, they will be forgiven... The prayer of the righteous person is powerful in what it can achieve.*
>
> (Jas. 5:13-16 CEB)

What a beautiful picture of the church! People pray for one another, sing together, confess to one another, and forgive one another. Some churches, even today, anoint the sick with oil as they pray over them. Of course, prayer is no guarantee that the sick will always be healed. We humans are mortal, after all. But many times, the Lord does restore the sick to health. And even when physical healing does not come, intercessory prayer for each other provides spiritual healing that is powerful in what it can achieve.

Exactly how prayer works is a mystery. But prayer that comes from faith is one of the most precious gifts we can offer each other. When we pray for one another, we are united by a common faith and in a common love. When we take one another to God in prayer, we are offering something beyond what we could do on a purely human level. There is great power in prayer.

THE POWER OF PRAYER
(Jas. 5:13-16)

I am not what you would call a frequent flyer, but Linda and I do travel on an airplane a few times a year. When we were returning from celebrating my mother's 90th birthday, I happened to look through one of those merchandise catalogues that airlines put in their seat pockets. The catalogues are filled with household gadgets, electronic toys, pet products, sports memorabilia, fashion accessories, and other novelty items. I have never ordered anything, but here are a few of the items that caught my eye:

- Collegiate Garden Gnome $19.99
- Lou Holtz signed 16x20 photo $159.99
- Picnic Cooler for 4 $124.95
- Picnic Basket for 2 $187.73
- Pooch Porch Potty $279.99
- Pet Ramp 3-step Staircase $199.95

Now, I am not saying these are bad products. Maybe you have one or more of them in your home. But I cannot see myself shelling out $159.99 for a signed photo of Lou Holtz, even if he is a former football coach at Notre Dame. And since we don't have a dog, we have no need for a Pooch Porch Potty or a Pet Ramp 3-step Staircase. Maybe a Collegiate Garden Gnome would look good in our yard, or then again, maybe not.

The item that really got my attention in the catalogue was a product called "The Human Slingshot." It's a big elastic band that can be used to sling people back and forth in a fast-paced game. And it can be yours for only $99.99, plus shipping, and it's available in blue or black. I can imagine that you are intrigued. Step inside the Human Slingshot with three of your closest friends, and then sling yourselves at each other. Apparently, the game goes on until someone falls and gets dragged through the dirt. Or even better, the game ends when there is a high-speed collision resulting in broken noses, limbs, ribs, and maybe even skulls. Here is my point: we really don't need to buy a human slingshot to get slung around. Most of us get slung around enough by life—and it is not a game.

Some years ago, a member of Village Baptist Church came to the Worship and Music Commission with an idea. He proposed that we put prayer cards in each pew pocket so that people in the congregation could write down their prayer requests. His thought was that the ushers could hand the prayer cards to me and I could read them during our concerns time, and then we could pray for the specific concerns. The Commission liked the idea of the prayer cards, but they could not figure out a way to get the cards to me before the concerns time. Instead, people would drop their prayer requests in the offering plate, and I would get the cards after the service. Then, during the week, I would pray for the requests on the cards. Sometimes the prayer requests would be mentioned the following Sunday. But more often, people would ask to keep their prayer requests confidential, so they were not shared in a public way.

I was very humbled to be entrusted with those concerns. Without betraying any confidences, I can mention their general nature. We received prayer requests for…

- healing, either for themselves or for a family member or friend
- job searches or interviews or other employment situations
- financial needs
- problems with an addiction or a mental health issue
- young people, that they might make wise decisions or seek a new direction
- the elderly, especially those who were dealing with a chronic medical condition
- persons receiving treatment for cancer or other serious illnesses
- those recovering from surgery
- troubled relationships
- help in grieving the loss of a loved one
- unspecified needs, where only a name was given, with no further information

Those prayer request cards were tangible reminders to me that we don't need a big elastic band to sling us around. Life slings us around plenty. Sometimes we feel like we've been knocked off our feet, thrown to the ground, and dragged through the dirt. Sometimes we collide with harsh realities—and it's not a game.

Every Monday morning, I would read through those prayer requests and pray for each one. I would keep the cards in my desk to remind me to pray for them throughout the week. Now, it's not that my prayers were any more powerful than the prayers of the people in the pews, nor that I had a hotline to God that was unavailable to them. But as their pastor, I was humbled to pray on their behalf. Praying for others is still one of the most important things I do as a minister of the gospel.

In chapter 5, James encourages his fellow Christians to pray. He encouraged them to pray for their own needs, to share their prayer requests with other believers, and to pray for one another, because "the prayer of the righteous is powerful and effective" (v. 16b). Just exactly what did James mean when he wrote, "the prayer of the righteous is powerful and effective"? Certainly, he was not suggesting that we will get everything we pray for. When my father was diagnosed with pancreatic cancer, we fervently prayed for his healing. But sometimes healing is not possible. Life has limits, and eventually we will all die from something. Yet, there is power in prayer.

Although we don't always get everything we pray for, many times we do. We pray for the sick, and they get well. We pray for comfort in the face of loss, and we find a way through our grief. We pray for strength in time of need, and that strength is given. Many times, God does answer our prayers in the way we want; other times, God answers our prayers in ways we never imagined. This is sometimes called the providence of God.

The providence of God means that God's ways are not our ways, and God's thoughts are not our thoughts. Sometimes what we want is not what God wants. Remember how Jesus prayed in the Garden of Gethsemane on the night before he died. With great anguish Jesus prayed that the cup of suffering would be taken from him. Clearly, he did not want to die on the cross. He fervently prayed that God would provide some other way. But at the end of his prayer Jesus prayed, "nevertheless, not what I want but what you want…your will be done."

In his book *A Scandalous Providence*, Frank Tupper noted that the word "providence" comes from the Latin word *providere*, which means "to provide." Tupper noted that *providere* has a double meaning. It's a combination of *pro*, which means "before," and *videre*, which means "sees." Thus, God sees before things happen. Because God has foreknowledge, God can provide for what is foreseen. In the providence of God, our needs will be provided for, no matter how unforeseen the events of life may be to us. Sometimes life is baffling and even overwhelming; we struggle to make sense of it. Sometimes it is hard to see the hand of God or to understand the purposes of God in difficult or painful or tragic circumstances. But God sees, and God knows, and God cares, and God provides.

There is great power in prayer. "The prayer of the righteous is powerful and effective." The power in prayer is not so much what prayer does for God, as what prayer can do for us. When we pray, we open ourselves to God's Spirit; we invite the peace of Christ into our hearts; we enter a dialogue with God that can change the way we look at life and change the way we live. The real power of prayer is that it connects us with God.

If we did not pray, if we did not need to pray, there would be no connection with God. And without that connection, our lives would have no ultimate purpose, and our deaths would be the end of us. Without that connection, "the slings and arrows of outrageous fortune" would have no meaning, and the sleep of death would be final. But when we pray, we are connected with a power far greater than ourselves, a power far greater than anything else in all creation.

Life is the ultimate human slingshot, but we can never fall beneath the everlasting arms of God, no matter how hard or how fast we fall. So, pray, pray, pray. Keep praying, in Jesus' name, pray. God will always hear, God will always be there, and God will always love. Pray.

PRAY FOR ONE ANOTHER
(Jas. 5:13-16)

I was a pastor for 45 years, but I've been visiting sick people and praying for them longer than that. As a senior in high school, I was selected to be "pastor" during Youth Week at our church. As part of my role, I went with the associate pastor when he made hospital visits. Dr. Roy DeBrand gave me some tips that I still practice today. For one thing, he taught me that if there were several people in the same hospital to visit, take the elevator to the highest floor and work your way down on foot. It's more efficient to take the stairs going down from floor to floor than to wait for the elevator. Plus, you get a little exercise along the way. Another thing Roy taught me was to wash my hands before and after each visit.

Roy also taught me never to sit on the patient's bed. Thus, I conduct most of my hospital visits standing up. Occasionally, I will sit in a chair if the patient is feeling well enough for a longer visit. But I never sit on the bed, unless the patient is sitting in a chair, and asks me to sit on the bed if there is no other chair available. Roy also taught me to keep my visits fairly brief. Most hospital patients need their rest, not some long, energy-sapping visit from their pastor. Finally, Roy taught me to offer a prayer at the end of the visit. Of course, there are times when a formal prayer is not appropriate, such as when the physician comes in. In those cases, I excuse myself and assure the patient that I will be praying for them. But most of the time, I conclude my visit with a prayer.

As I said, I made my first hospital visits more than 50 years ago, and I've been visiting patients in the hospital ever since. I made hospital visits when I was a youth minister in college, when I was a pastoral intern in seminary, and when I served as associate pastor of a church in Silver Spring, Maryland. And, as pastor of Village Baptist Church in Bowie, Maryland for 33 years, I made countless hospital visits and nursing home visits. Visiting people in the hospital and praying for them has always been an important part of my ministry.

James 5 instructs us to pray for one another, especially in times of illness or distress. Prayer was vitally important in the first century when there were few medical resources. Imagine living in a time before antibiotics, anesthesia, X-rays, MRIs, and other medical treatments and procedures. When people got sick back then, about all they could do was pray. Not only could Christians pray for themselves, but they could also call upon the church to pray for them. Because there were no hospitals, sick people generally stayed at home. It would not have been practical for the entire congregation to go to a person's home to pray at their bedside, so representatives from the church would gather to pray over a sick person. In James' church, those representatives were called elders.

James was the leader of the church in Jerusalem, comprised mainly of Christians from a Jewish background. The Jews were familiar with elders. The title refers more to positions of respect rather than age. Elders were leaders in the Jewish religion, along with scribes and Pharisees and priests. So, it was natural for the church in Jerusalem to appoint elders.

In other churches the leaders were called bishops and deacons. Bishops were pastoral overseers, and deacons helped to carry out the benevolent ministries of the church. The elders in James' church in Jerusalem functioned as deacons. When someone in the church was sick, the elders would gather at their bedside and pray over them and anoint them with oil.

The anointing with oil served two purposes. In some cases, oil was used as a kind of medicinal treatment. For example, the good Samaritan in Luke 10 who stopped to help the wounded man by the side of the road anointed his wounds with oil and then wrapped them in bandages. Oil was sometimes used as a soothing agent to dress wounds. Anointing with oil also had symbolic significance.

In the Old Testament, kings and prophets were anointed with oil to set them apart for God's service and to symbolize God's presence with them. Anointing a sick person with oil might have been a symbolic ritual to set the patient apart for God's special attention and care. Some churches today, especially charismatic churches, anoint a sick person with oil and then pray over them. It is not that the oil itself has any miraculous powers, but it is a powerful symbol of God's presence and care.

The father of one of our church members was in the last stage of ALS disease. He indicated to his daughter that he wanted to be baptized before he died. One of our deacons went with me to the hospital to baptize him. Because he was confined to the bed, baptism by immersion was not possible. The deacon assisted me by holding a basin while I sprinkled water on his head. Then we said a prayer over him, and I anointed his head with oil as a sign of God's blessing and presence in his life. Although he was almost completely paralyzed, the man was fully aware of what was going on. It was obvious to all of us who were gathered around his bed that the baptism and anointing were deeply meaningful to him. He passed away just a few days after his baptism and anointing.

Every Sunday during worship at Village Baptist church we had a time of prayer for the sick and others with needs. We didn't gather around them and pray over them, but we prayed for them in worship. Sometimes when I would visit sick people for whom we had prayed, I would tell them that we had prayed for them. The response was always one of deep gratitude. One usual response was, "Thanks: I need all the prayers I can get!" James said, "prayer that comes from faith will heal the sick." Of course, this does not mean that every sick person will get well. Sometimes healing is not possible. But that does not stop us from praying.

In 2 Corinthians 12 Paul wrote about a "thorn in the flesh" that brought great suffering into his life. We don't know what his "thorn in the flesh" was. Maybe it was failing eyesight or migraine headaches or epileptic seizures or recurrences of malaria. All those have been suggested as possible maladies Paul was dealing with. It seems to have been a chronic condition, however, because Paul repeatedly and fervently prayed that it would be removed from him. Paul prayed, but he was not healed. Paul wrote, "Three times I appealed to the Lord about this, that it would leave me, but he said to me, 'My grace is sufficient for you, for power is made perfect in weakness'" (2 Cor. 12:8-9). Sometimes we pray and healing does not come. But the promise is still true: "the Lord will restore them to health." The healing may not come on this side of eternity, but in the end all will be well.

As I said, it is a mistake to think that every prayer for the sick will result in physical healing. But it is also a mistake to think that prayer for the sick won't do any good. It is a great encouragement for those who are sick to know that other Christians are praying for them. Often, healing does come. I can't explain how it works, but people who are prayed for tend to do better than those who are not prayed for. There is a power in prayer that is mysterious and inexplicable. Maybe it has to do with coming alongside God in prayer. When we align our wills with God's will, miracles can happen—not every time and not under our control, but miracles can happen. In a sense, every healing is a miracle. God created us in such a way that our bodies can and often do overcome illnesses and injuries. As Hawkeye Pierce said on the *M*A*S*H* television show, "God cures the patient, and the doctor collects the fee."

The older you get, the more you realize how precious and fragile life is. When you get sick, call upon the church and the church people will pray for you. If you know someone who is ill, share that concern with others who might pray for them. Sometimes the best we can do is to pray.

THE POWER OF PRAYER
(Jas. 5:13-16)

I received a call from a reporter with *The Washington Post* who had done a story after the Village Baptist Church building had burned, and then kept in touch from time to time to see how we were doing. This call, however, was not to check on the status of our building, but to ask me a theological question. He was doing research for an article for the newspaper, and he wanted to ask my opinion about "the power of prayer in times of crisis." He mentioned several incidents that had happened recently—a train derailment in the metro area, trapped miners in Pennsylvania, and a deadly tornado in southern Maryland. He asked about the role of prayer in such times.

It turned out that his article appeared in the newspaper without my input. The reporter had called on a Saturday afternoon when I was not in the church office, so he had left a message on the answering machine. By the time I got back to him, it was past his deadline for the article. He did talk with some other pastors, though, and with some people who were involved in those crisis events. He reported some powerful testimonies from people who called on God "while standing in the shadow of death," for example:

- After the train derailment, an Amtrak conductor dropped to his knees and prayed for God's help. He and more than 100 other people on the train were injured, but miraculously no one was killed.
- During the rescue effort at the mine in Somerset, Pennsylvania, ministers led family members in prayer for the nine coal miners who were trapped below. Again, miraculously, every miner was saved.
- In southern Maryland, a father recited the Lord's Prayer as he huddled on the floor with his family while the tornado passed outside their living room window, sparing their house but destroying all other buildings on their block. That family was miraculously saved, but others were not so blessed.

The reporter asked the question, "What do these testimonies mean? In a crisis situation, do the chances of survival increase if you ask God to save you?"

No doubt, the people who prayed to God during those crisis moments and were spared serious injury or death believe that God intervened on their behalf and saved them. But we know that God does not intervene every time people pray for deliverance. At least five people were killed by the tornado that passed through southern Maryland, and some of them may have been praying too. I have prayed beside the hospital beds of many patients over the years, and most of those people got well, but a few did not. As Christians, we believe that God always hears and answers our prayers. Many times, God does intervene and work a miracle of deliverance or healing. But sometimes, it seems that God's answer is "no." What then can we say about the power of prayer?

The Bible has a lot to say about prayer. James 5 advises Christians to pray at all times and in all circumstances. Like Paul, who said we are to "pray without ceasing" (1 Thess. 5:17), James wrote that every situation in life should be an occasion for prayer, and gave some specific examples.

First, James said that we should pray in times of suffering: "if any of you are suffering, they should pray" (Jas. 5:13). This almost goes without saying. In times of suffering, our first instinct is to pray. The word used here for suffering connotes emotional distress or depression or anxiety as a result of some negative life experience.

I will never forget that first Sunday after the fire that destroyed our church building. We gathered in the parking lot before our burned building, with the smell of smoke still in the air. We prayed together, and then went to the nearby fire station community room to continue our worship. We were all in shock, and grieving, but we found the strength we needed by holding on to one another and reaching out to God in prayer. I don't think I've ever hugged as many people as I did that first Sunday after the fire. But it wasn't just the hugs that got us through that difficult time. It was the sure conviction that God was with us and that God would see us through. In times of suffering, the first and best thing we can do is turn to God in prayer.

James also said that we should pray in good times as well as bad. "If any of you are happy, they should sing" (Jas. 5:13). Singing songs of praise is a form of prayer. There is a hymn written by Novella D. Preston Jordan (1901–1991) that says:

> My singing is a prayer, O Lord,
> A prayer of thanks and praise;
> In music, Lord, I worship Thee;
> Thy beauty fills my days.

Too often during the good times of life we are apt to forget about God. But God wants to be a part of our lives just as much during those times when we are happy as he does when we are sad.

On the first Sunday after our church's fire, as we stood in the parking lot, I began our worship by quoting a verse from Psalms: "This is the day the Lord has made; let us rejoice and be glad in it" (118:24). I chose that verse precisely because it was the opposite of how most of us were feeling. But we needed to be reminded in that dark time that each day is a gift from God, and that God has blessed us in many ways.

After 34 months, on the Sunday that we finally re-entered our new church building, we processed down the street from our temporary meeting place to the new structure on our church property. As we processed, one of our musicians played "When the Saints Go Marching In" on his saxophone. That song set the tone for our rejoicing. Then when we reached the building, before we went inside, we assembled in the parking lot and prayed. Except that time, we prayed with great rejoicing. Our spirits finally matched the spirit of the psalm. When we finally entered the sanctuary, there was plenty of singing!

Third, James said we should pray when we are sick. Not only are we to pray for ourselves, but we also are to pray for each other. The health care system of the first century was limited. Average life expectancy was 20–30 years. That sounds extremely low because some people lived into their 60s and 70s and beyond, but the infant mortality rate was exceptionally high. According to one scholar, probably more than 25 percent of all children died within their first year of life, and about 50 percent of all children died before the age of 10. Within large cities, malnutrition was a constant cause of illness, along with the spread of infectious diseases. Bladder stones, rickets, and certain eye ailments afflicted all levels of society. When people got sick, there was little medical care.

According to researcher Ralph Jackson, because "both doctors and drugs were of uncertain quality, few illnesses were easily cured." If a Greek physician in the tradition of Hippocrates were available, he didn't come cheap, and it might take days for him to give a diagnosis. Other sick people resorted to local shamans and folk medicine practitioners who provided treatment through potions and incantations and remedies of questionable value. Sometimes sick people were carried to the shrines of gods or goddesses to make offerings and pray for healing. More often, taking care of the sick was a family matter. The head of the family or other family members would use herbs and charms to try to make the sick person well.[1]

In contrast to the common methods of treating the sick in his day, James prescribed a different remedy: call the elders of the church to come and pray over them, anointing them with oil in the name of the Lord. Taking care of the sick became one of the major ministries of the early church. Instead of charging exorbitant fees or applying remedies that might do more harm than good, church members would offer practical help and pray for those who were ill. Sometimes the sick person would be anointed with oil as a sign of God's presence and help. The olive oil may have had some medicinal value, but more important was its symbolic value as a spiritual palliative. Elders and other leaders in the church would come to the sick person's bedside and provide both spiritual and physical comfort and support. Sometimes the sick were physically healed through those prayers of faith. In every case, they were surrounded by the love of the church and the grace of God.

James mentions a fourth occasion for prayer: when we sin. God is always ready to forgive, but we must pray to God and ask for his forgiveness in order to receive the grace he wants to give. James says to "confess your sins to each other and pray for each other" (Jas. 5:16). We are not in the habit of confessing our sins to each other. Oh, we know that we are all sinners, but when it comes to identifying specific sins, we would rather deal in generalities. It would be a rare church where people could be so honest with each other as to confess their specific sins to one another. But if they did that, I dare say it would result not only in forgiveness, but also in change. If I confessed my sin of uncontrolled anger, I would feel some sense of accountability to address that sin in my own life. If Jesus is our Savior and Lord, he saves us from our sins and gives us the power to live saved lives. That does not mean we will never mess up, but it means we will spend more of our lives following his will than following our own.

So, James said to pray at all times: Pray when you are in distress, pray when you are glad, pray when you are sick, pray when you sin. But what about the original question? Does prayer really work? Can we really count on prayer to save us in those crisis situations of life? I would answer with another question: What else do we have to count on but God? There is great power in prayer—sometimes power to change circumstances, always power to change us.

Our new church building was equipped with a fire-suppression sprinkler system. But the new system did not work until it was tied to the main water line that runs along the road in front of the church. We had a connecting water line providing service to the old building, but that line was not large enough to supply water for the sprinkler system. So, we had to install a new, larger water line to connect the main line at the street with the building. The new line provided enough water for daily use and to put out a fire should another crisis ever occur.

Prayer is our connecting line to God, providing all the power we need for daily living, and extra power in those crisis situations of life. Prayer is our conduit through which the grace and power of God flow into our lives. Every time we pray, we let the healing waters flow.

QUESTIONS FOR DISCUSSION/REFLECTION

1. If God already knows our hearts, why is it necessary to pray?
2. What is the purpose of praying for each other?
3. What do we say if prayer does not heal the sick?
4. How do you feel about confessing your sins to others?
5. In what ways is the prayer of the righteous person powerful?

NOTE

[1] "Some New Angles on James 5:13-20," *Review and Expositor*, 97 (2000), 208.

CHAPTER 8

NEW BIRTH INTO A LIVING HOPE
(1 Peter 1:3-9)

> *Praise be to the God and Father of our Lord Jesus Christ! In his great mercy he has given us new birth into a living hope through the resurrection of Jesus Christ from the dead.... In all this you greatly rejoice, though now for a little while you may have had to suffer grief in all kinds of trials....for you are receiving the end result of your faith, the salvation of your souls.*
>
> (1 Pet. 1:3, 6, 9 NIV)

The First Letter of Peter was written to encourage Christians in Asia Minor who were experiencing suffering in all kinds of trials because of their commitment to Jesus Christ. They likely were "second generation" Christians who had not met Jesus in person, but who had become his followers through the testimony of others. Even though they could not see him, they believed in him and were "filled with an inexpressible and glorious joy."

This joy is founded on the resurrection of Jesus Christ from the dead, and the "new birth" that comes through faith, and the "living hope" for what is yet to come. The ultimate result is "the salvation of your souls." Through their suffering, the quality of their faith is revealed, a quality of greater value than gold. As adherents of an often-misunderstood religion, Christians must expect to suffer persecution and social ostracism. Yet, the difficulties of the Christian life diminish when compared with the spiritual riches of God's great mercy.

THE OUTCOME OF YOUR FAITH
(1 Pet. 1:3-9)

I love to hear about people who make the best of whatever life may bring. Courtland Milloy writes a regular column for *The Washington Post*. In a column after the death of his mother, Courtland wrote a tribute to his father, age 90. His father lost his wife, Courtland's mother, when she died at the age of 87. In reality, he started losing her even before her death, as she started showing signs of dementia. Despite her increasing disability, he remained devoted to her.

When he became convinced that she should not drive any more, he took her car keys and hid them. He said he had to endure the worst scolding of his life. He told Courtland, "Taking her keys was the hardest thing I've ever done." It was the hardest thing because he respected his wife so much. It was the hardest thing he had ever done, until he had to say goodbye to her for the final time. The Sunday after she died, Courtland's father went to church, Bible in hand. He confessed, "I really don't feel like going, but I need to." With God's help, he was going to make the best of whatever life would bring.

Tiffani Blackwell met Jerrell Ellerbe on a dating web site. Both in their late 20s, Tiffani was an elementary special education teacher in Arlington County, Virginia, and Jerrell was a Park Police officer in Prince George's County, Maryland. After weeks of trading messages and talking on the phone, they finally met for coffee in Old Town Alexandria. It was Super Bowl Sunday 2013. They clicked, and it did not take long for Tiffani and Jerrell to become a couple. In addition to being attracted to each other, they discovered they shared many of the same values, such as dedication to family and a commitment to their work. Two years later, in March of 2015, they became engaged. They set their wedding date for March of 2016.

But six months after their engagement, Tiffani suffered a massive stroke. She was only 31 years old at the time. What began as a splitting headache quickly escalated into vertigo, blurred vision, and slurred speech. It took three trips to the hospital before the doctors finally diagnosed what was wrong with her. Jerrell and everyone who knew her were devastated. Jerrell said, "They told us it was on the brain stem and most of the time people end up permanently disabled or die." Jerrell and Tiffani's parents didn't give up. They made it their focus to give Tiffani all the support they could to help her recover.

Recovery was a long and slow road. Tiffani remained in the hospital for a month, undergoing brain therapy for up to eight hours a day. She had to re-learn how to do basic tasks, such as signing her name, singing a song, and climbing a flight of stairs. Most nights, Jerrell or Tiffani's dad slept on a stiff plastic cot beside her hospital bed. Seven months after her stroke, Tiffani had made amazing progress. She still had difficulty reading, driving, and writing, but she could talk fluidly, and she could walk without assistance. Jerrell said, "She keeps fighting. Every day is a fight to get her life back to normal." Incredibly, Tiffani and Jerrell were able to keep their wedding date.

On March 19, 2016 Tiffani Blackwell walked down the aisle and joined hands with Jerrell Ellerbe. They promised to "have and to hold, for better or for worse, in sickness and in health," as long as they both shall live. Jerrell wrote a self-published book about their experiences, hoping to inspire others and to raise awareness about strokes.

How do people make the best of whatever life may bring? Well, a lot of it has to do with faith. In his first letter, Peter wrote about the difference that faith can make in our lives. After the salutation, in which Peter introduced himself and addressed the recipients of his letter, he wrote: "Blessed be the God and Father of our Lord Jesus Christ! By his great mercy he has given us a new birth into a living hope through the resurrection of Jesus Christ from the dead" (1:3). Peter was not oblivious to the problems of life. He continued in verse 6: "In this you rejoice, even if now for a little while you have had to suffer various trials." Peter knew that life is not always easy.

Sometimes life is hard. But it is because we have a new birth into a living hope through the resurrection of Jesus Christ from the dead that the hard things of life do not have to be the final word. Sometimes the hard things of life can change our lives for the better.

New Birth Into a Living Hope

Jim Rendon, author of the book, *Upside: The New Science of Post-Traumatic Growth*, acknowledges that most everyone hopes to avoid the hard things of life. We hope to avoid things such as loss, illness, accidents, violence, and other traumas. Unfortunately, most of us are not so fortunate. Scientists who have studied such things calculate that an estimated 75 percent of us will experience at least one major traumatic event in our lives. Such times can cause great suffering, but they can also lead to great growth.

Two psychologists surveyed about 600 survivors of traumatic events. Not surprising, most of the survivors reported experiencing negative effects from those events. But to the surprise of the researchers, many survivors also reported positive changes. Those changes included developing greater inner strength, becoming closer to family and friends, and reorienting their lives toward more fulfilling goals. Their suffering served as a catalyst to make positive changes in their lives. The researchers found that not only did many of those survivors of traumatic events experience healing, but they also experienced growth. They became new and better versions of themselves.

In her book, *One Thousand Gifts*, Ann Voskamp asks: "Who would ever know the greater graces of comfort and perseverance, mercy and forgiveness, patience and courage, if no shadows fell over a life?"[1] No one wants to suffer trials. But for most people, trials come whether we want them or not. This is where our faith can make a difference. We who believe in Jesus believe that something good can come out of something bad. After Jesus died on the cross, something good came out of something bad. "By his great mercy he has given us a new birth into a living hope through the resurrection of Jesus Christ from the dead" (1 Pet. 1:3b). The outcome of our faith is a new birth and a living hope.

It is not events that determine the course of our lives, but rather how we respond to the events. In the early 20th century, Ella Wheeler Wilcox wrote the poem, "The Winds of Fate":

One ship drives east and another drives west
With the selfsame winds that blow
It's the set of the sails and not the gales
That tells the way to go

Like the winds of the seas are the ways of fate
As we voyage along through life
It's the set of the soul that decides its goal
And not the calm or the strife.

When Tiffani Blackwell and Jerrell Ellerbe were married, there was hardly a dry eye in the room. For some couples, the high point of the ceremony is the vows, or the exchange of rings, or the kiss. But for Jerrell, the high point of the ceremony was just seeing Tiffani walk down the aisle. After all they had been through, especially when there was no guarantee she would ever walk again, seeing his bride walk down the aisle was like a new birth into a living hope. "Now look at her," Jerrell thought: "How lucky are we to have this moment?"[2]

Our faith can help us to make the best of whatever life may bring. The bread and the cup of Communion remind us how something good can come out of something bad. They remind us that God is at work in even the most tragic events of life to bring blessing out of them. Through Jesus we are receiving the outcome of our faith, the salvation of our souls. Although we have not seen him, we love him. And even though we do not see him now, we believe in him and rejoice with an indescribable and glorious joy. It's not the gales but the set of our sails as we voyage along through life. It's the set of the soul that decides our goal. By faith, God will see us through.

FOOTSTEPS IN THE CONCRETE
(1 Pet. 1:1-9)

The week after the Village Baptist Church building burned in January of 2000, a group of us met with our insurance company representative to try to figure out what to do next. The claims agent told us that it would take at least a year to rebuild. When he said, "at least a year," I thought to myself, "surely it won't take that long!" Thank God, I did not know then that it would take more than three years. One of the problems was that a lot of the work had to be done more than once.

The kitchen door, the door to the church office, the door next to the organ, the entire doorway going into the west wing, several windows, and the carpeting in the foyer all had to be replaced. It took three tries to get the baptistry to hold water. The sidewalk had to be torn up and replaced. The front steps had to be replaced after we discovered that one of them had a low spot that held water. The concrete contractor tried grinding down the edges and putting a surface coating over the low spot, but that only made matters worse. So, a member of our church sent a crew to rip out the old "new" steps, and the concrete contractor poured new "new" steps. That was on a Thursday.

There was a lot of activity in our new church building on Thursday afternoons and evenings. A mental health counselor saw clients in her office at the end of one hallway. The adult choir rehearsed in the sanctuary on Thursday nights. The handbell choir rehearsed in the fellowship hall. A CDA (Chemically Dependent Anonymous) group met in the church parlor. And the Mitchellville Community School of the Arts offered music lessons and art classes in the educational wing.

The area around the newly poured concrete steps was marked off with orange barrels and yellow construction tape, but that did not stop one little boy from bounding up the steps before anyone could stop him—and leaving footprints in the wet cement. Apparently, he spotted his violin teacher, and he was so excited to greet her that he did not notice the barrels and the tape and the wet concrete.

A member of our church who works in construction was there that night, and he did his best to smooth out the footprints the little boy had made. The mother of the child who left his mark was greatly apologetic and offered to pay for the repairs, but the damage was done. When I inspected the steps the next morning, the outlines of a child's shoeprints were clearly visible, but it was not as bad as I had feared. The director of the Mitchellville Community School of the Arts came by to explain what had happened and to apologize and to reiterate the mother's apology and offer to pay for the damage.

New Birth Into a Living Hope

Over time, as the concrete hardened, the footprints became less noticeable. If you stood on the front porch and looked out toward the parking lot, you could see the outline of a couple of shoeprints on the top two steps, but it was nothing to worry about. But the incident became for me a kind of parable of life. Let me share some of the lessons I learned.

Life seldom unfolds exactly according to plan.

We learned a lot over the three years that it took to reconstruct our church building. A lot of things went wrong and did not unfold according to plan. Just about every person at one time or another has to deal with unplanned-for and unforeseen and unwanted circumstances. Whether it is financial setbacks or job losses, health problems, the death of a loved one, a marital breakup, or the estrangement of family members, eventually just about every one of us experiences life not unfolding according to plan.

Peter wrote about this reality in the opening of his first letter, alludeing to "all kinds of trials" his readers had suffered, and to their faith being tested. Complications, trials, and troubles come into every life. That is true even for people who believe in God and who seek to follow Christ. Like a scratch on a new car, or a stain on the new carpet, or footprints on the new concrete, the quest for perfection is marred by the reality of life in the world.

Sooner or later, someone is going to leave footprints in the concrete.

Sometimes deliberately, but more often unintentionally, we step in each other's wet cement. As Paul said in Romans 3:23: "all have sinned and fallen short of the glory of God." Sometimes we say or do things to mess up other people's lives, and sometimes it's the people who are closest to us. Someone has said, "Experience is a wonderful thing. It enables you to recognize a mistake when you make it again."

Peter did not specify exactly what caused his readers to "suffer grief in all kinds of trials," but he viewed those experiences as a means to prove the genuineness of their faith. Peter himself would suffer his own trials, leading up to his martyrdom in Rome, traditionally dated around A.D. 64.

It was a time when many Christians would suffer at the hands of the Roman emperor Nero. According to the Roman historian Tacitus, Nero blamed the devasting fire in Rome on the Christians, and he had many arrested and brutally executed by "being thrown to the beasts, crucified, and burned alive." According to later church teachings, Peter was crucified upside down, because he did not feel worthy to die in the same manner as his Lord Jesus Christ. Yet, Peter placed the present-day sufferings into the larger context of the imperishable inheritance "kept in heaven for you."

The footprints in the concrete can be redeemed

Peter wrote about the redemptive power of faith. Life seldom unfolds according to plan, but God by his great mercy "has given us new birth into a living hope through the resurrection of Jesus Christ from the dead." No matter how messed up life can get, God wants to fill us with an "inexpressible and glorious joy," a joy not based on the external circumstances of our lives, but a joy based on the gift of salvation and the hope of heaven. We may not recognize it at the time, but God is at work in all circumstances to bring good out of them.

I was showing the footprints on the front steps to a lady from another church. Upon seeing them she remarked, "What a wonderful testimony!" I thought to myself, "That's a strange way to look at it." She went on to explain: "Those footprints say a lot about your church. They are a sign to everyone that this is a church that welcomes children."

How right she was! The new building was not constructed to be a monument that would stand forever in perfect completion. It was constructed to be a center of ministry, alive with the laughter and energy of children, filled with the sounds of music and fellowship and worship and prayer. From that moment on, every time I would go up those front steps and see those footprints, I would be reminded of why the church building was there. It was there not to build a monument for ourselves, but to serve others in Christ's name. We were there to say to little children, "There is a place here for you." Jesus said, "Let the children come to me, and do not hinder them, for to such belong the Kingdom of God" (Mark 10:14).

Life seldom unfolds according to plan, and sometimes people step in our wet cement. But ours is a God who redeems those footprints in the concrete and gives us a new birth into a living hope. What more do we need?

BLACK SWANS AND THE LOVE OF GOD
(1 Pet. 1:3-9)

Most of us remember where we were on September 11, 2001. Linda and I were in Wisconsin, on vacation with my parents. We were enjoying our stay at Green Lake Conference Center on beautiful Green Lake. The day before, on September 10, we had played golf with Ken Giacoletto, the president of Green Lake. On the morning of September 11, Ken was going to give us a guided tour of the sprawling campus of the conference center.

It was just before 8:00 a.m. Central time when my father turned on the television in our hotel suite. He summoned us to come see what was happening. The first tower of the World Trade Center in New York City was on fire. We watched in shock and horror as the second tower was struck by another airplane. It was unbelievable! Then there were reports of another plane that had flown into the Pentagon, and yet a fourth airplane that had been hijacked.

By this time, people were jumping out of windows in the World Trade Center towers, preferring to die from falling rather than to be suffocated from smoke or consumed by fire. It was too horrible to watch, but we could not turn away. Then the Twin Towers came down, first the South Tower, then the North Tower. Again, it was horrifying to see, but we kept watching, half a country away, safe and secure on the top floor of the Roger Williams Inn along the beautiful and peaceful shores of Green Lake.

September 11, 2001 was a day we will never forget. Nassim Nicholas Taleb, a finance professor and former Wall Street trader, calls what happened on 9/11 a "black swan" event. Taleb notes that before Europeans happened upon Australia, people in the

New Birth Into a Living Hope

Old World believed that all swans were white. The discovery of a black swan was an unexpected and surprising event. Taleb uses the metaphor of the black swan to connote any event or occurrence that deviates from what is usually expected and is therefore difficult to predict.

In his book, *The Black Swan: The Impact of the Highly Improbable*, Taleb writes that a black swan is an event with three attributes. First, it is an outlier, meaning "it lies outside the realm of regular expectations, because nothing in the past can convincingly point to its possibility." Second, "it carries an extreme impact." Third, we "concoct explanations for its occurrence after the fact, making it explainable and predictable."[3] Thus, there are three characteristics of a black swan event: rarity, impact, and retrospective predictability.

The terrorist attack on 9/11 was a black swan event. No one saw it coming, although in retrospect we should have. If we had been expecting it, then armed fighter jets would have been circling over Manhattan and Washington that morning, and commercial aircraft cockpits would have been equipped with locked bulletproof doors. Instead, the first two jets that were scrambled to intercept the hijacked airliner over Pennsylvania were unarmed. The pilots were intending to ram the aircraft to bring it down. Instead, it was the passengers themselves aboard Flight 93 who heroically intervened, at the cost of their own lives.

Since 9/11 we are a little better when it comes to expecting the unexpected, but not really. We will never completely eliminate black swans. Life is full of uncertainties, and it is impossible to predict or expect every event that might occur.

The book of 1 Peter was supposedly written by the apostle Peter sometime before he was martyred in Rome around AD 64. The recipients of his letter were Christians living in Asia Minor, many of them Gentiles, resident aliens, and household slaves. Part of Peter's message to these Christians was to expect the unexpected. He wrote to encourage them to be prepared for possible persecution, or at least to expect social ostracism, because of their faith in Christ. In chapter 1, Peter alludes to suffering various trials and to faith tested by fire. Peter knew firsthand what he was writing about. Early church traditions say that Peter died during the persecution of Christians by Emperor Nero. Yet even though Peter suffered mightily, he did not lose heart. And he wrote to encourage his fellow Christians not to lose heart, even in the face of unexpected events that would have a major impact upon their lives.

After 9/11 our worldview changed. I remember how shaken we were after 9/11, how wounded and vulnerable we all felt. There was a fresh upsurge of patriotism in our country, and a renewed return to faith. Two days after 9/11, as excavators were digging through the rubble of the World Trade Center, one man spotted a steel T-beam standing upright amid the twisted debris. It was a massive form of metal, about 17-feet tall and weighing more than two tons, in the shape of a cross. A few days later he pointed out this strange phenomenon to a Catholic priest who was blessing remains at Ground Zero. The priest persuaded city officials to allow a crew of volunteer union workers to raise it out of the wreckage with a crane and mount it on a concrete pedestal. The priest viewed this T-beam cross as a revelation, a sign that "God had not abandoned Ground Zero."

The cross at Ground Zero became a gathering place for remembrance and prayer. Each week the priest would return to hold services there. Crew members and family members of the victims would come together to pray. Eventually, as work continued at the site, the World Trade Center cross was moved to a nearby church for temporary safekeeping. Later it was moved again to the National September 11 Memorial and Museum in lower Manhattan. Once a part of the wreckage, the cross is now a symbol of remembrance, and a sign of healing and hope.

The black swan of 9/11 has had an enormous impact on our nation and the world. It has affected how we look at life, our sense of safety and security, our peace of mind, our confidence in the future. The black swan of 9/11 has reminded us that our only ultimate security, the only thing we can really count on, the only reality we can predict with certainty, is the steadfast love of God. As the Psalmist said, "God is our refuge and strength, a very present help in trouble. Therefore we will not fear, though the earth should change, though the mountains shake in the heart of the sea" (Ps. 46:1-2).

Not all black swans are bad, though. Who could have predicted the fall of the Soviet Union or the rise of the Internet? Sometimes unexpected events bring about great good. The death of Jesus on the cross was a black swan. No one could have predicted it, except Jesus himself. The Resurrection was a black swan. No one expected Jesus to rise from the grave. Even his closest disciples did not believe it at first. But such unexpected events have had a profound impact on the course of human destiny and on our individual lives. Peter said that because we believe in Jesus, we "are filled with an inexpressible and glorious joy;" for we are receiving the end result of our faith, the salvation of our souls.

We cannot predict black swans, but about this we can predict, for sure: the steadfast love of the Lord never ceases. His mercies never end. Great is God's faithfulness.

QUESTIONS FOR DISCUSSION/REFLECTION

1. What is the "new birth into a living hope"?
2. What kind of trials have you had to suffer?
3. How do trials prove the genuineness of our faith?
4. How can you allow your faith to fill you with "an inexpressible and glorious joy"?
5. What is "the end result" of our faith? Hint: the salvation of our souls. What does that mean for you?

NOTES

[1] Ann Voskamp, *One Thousand Gifts: A Dare to Live Fully Right Where You Are* (Zondervan, 2011), 71.

[2] The story of Tiffani Blackwell and Jerrell Ellerbe was reported in *The Washington Post*, April 3, 2016, E14.

[3] Nassim Taleb, *The Black Swan: The Impact of the Highly Improbable* (Penguin, 2008), 1.

CHAPTER 9

THE HOPE THAT IS IN YOU
(1 Peter 3:8-9, 15b-18)

Finally, all of you, have unity of spirit, sympathy, love for one another, a tender heart, and a humble mind. Do not repay evil for evil or abuse for abuse; but, on the contrary, repay with a blessing. Always be ready to make your defense to anyone who demands from you an accounting for the hope that is in you…

(1 Pet. 3:8-9a, 15b NRSV)

Love for one another is the defining characteristic of the Christian life. Instead of seeking revenge for wrongs against us, we offer forgiveness. A tender heart and a humble mind lead us to repay evil and abuse with blessing. Our example is Christ. He suffered for our sins, to bring us to God. He died for us, but death could not hold him, for he rose to new life. That is the hope within us. Paul explained the significance of Jesus' resurrection in 1 Corinthians 15:22 when he said, "for as all die in Adam, so all will be made alive in Christ." Because our future is secure, those who suffer for doing good will inherit a blessing.

THE HOPE THAT IS IN YOU, PART 1
(1 Pet. 3:8-17)

The people in Oklahoma were recovering from devastating tornadoes that struck their state. The city of Moore looked like a war zone. Entire neighborhoods were reduced to rubble, two elementary schools were destroyed, and the local hospital looked like a bomb had hit it. Tragically, more than two dozen people lost their lives, and hundreds were injured. Even more tragic, that same community had been struck by deadly tornadoes before, twice within 14 years.

In the aftermath of natural disasters, people tend to ask theological questions: Why did this happen? Why does God allow tornadoes to harm some people and spare others? According to *Time* magazine, "the cyclone was arbitrary. Within yards of a house in matchsticks, one could find a china cabinet undisturbed, every fragile plate intact." *Time* concluded, the tornado "reminded thousands of people what really mattered."[1]

After the tornado in Oklahoma, a woman was being interviewed on television in front of her leveled house. She expressed gratitude that she had survived, but was grieving that she could not find her beloved dog, a miniature schnauzer that had been ripped from her arms as she had huddled in the bathroom. As the woman was talking, someone noticed something moving beneath the rubble behind her. The camera panned down to her collapsed house, and sure enough, it was her dog sticking out its nose from the debris. The woman was overcome with emotion. She immediately started to lift boards and pieces of drywall to try to free her pet. Someone off camera reached in and helped her remove the heavy materials and lift the dog out. The woman started stroking her beloved pup, wet and ragged, but apparently unharmed. With tears in her eyes the woman said, "I thought God answered just one prayer, 'Let me be okay.' He answered both of them."[2]

Later, CNN reporter Wolf Blitzer was interviewing a woman whose house had been destroyed. Her husband was not home when the tornado struck. He had called and told her to get into the bathtub with their 18-month-old son, and to cover themselves with a mattress. For a time, that's what the woman did. She and her son were huddled in the bathtub with a mattress over them. But as she watched weather reports on her computer, she saw that the tornado was heading right for their street. The woman made a quick decision that likely saved their lives.

Instead of "sheltering in place," she grabbed her son and ran barefoot out of the house. She jumped into her car with her son on her lap. She didn't even take time to buckle him into his car seat. She drove south because the tornado was heading northeast. About a mile away she stopped just long enough to put her son in his car seat. Then she kept driving south and listening to the weather report on the radio. Finally, after the tornado had passed, she turned the car around and headed back home.

By the time she got there, her husband was frantically digging through the rubble looking for her and their child. He was afraid they were buried inside because he had told them to hunker down in the bathtub. He noticed that their car was gone, but a lot of cars were gone. Their neighbor's car had been blown into another neighbor's yard. As far as he knew, their car was blown away and his wife and child were somewhere under the destroyed house. Needless to say, there was a joyous reunion when he saw that they were okay.

After hearing this incredible story, Wolf Blitzer asked the woman if she was thanking the Lord for their deliverance. She didn't reply, so he asked her again, if she was thanking the Lord they had survived. Finally, with kind of a sheepish look on her face, the woman admitted that she was an atheist. She didn't believe in God, so she had no reason to give thanks. Wolf had a puzzled look on his face. It certainly wasn't the answer he was expecting to his question. Wolf finally said, "All right, don't thank the Lord."

Two interviews with survivors of the deadly tornado—two very different ways of interpreting what had happened: One woman said that her prayers had been answered, both for her own safety, and for the safety of her beloved dog. Another woman was glad that she and her son and her husband were alive, but she did not thank the Lord for their survival because she doesn't believe in God. That second woman is in a minority in our country.

Even though one in five Americans say they have no religion, the majority of Americans still say they believe in God. But the number of religiously affiliated is decreasing, in part because many Americans are disillusioned by religion, or they don't see the need for it. Even people who were raised in the church and in Christian homes are dropping out, or only occasionally attending religious services. Someone has labeled them "C & E Christians," meaning they go to church only at Christmas and Easter. But can we understand our lives and the world around us apart from religion?

The word "religion" comes from the Latin term *religio*, which means "awe or fear of a god or spirit." Most religions believe there is a greater reality, whether a god or a spirit or a supernatural realm. And most religions attempt to address the ultimate questions of life. It is natural to ask those ultimate questions: Where did we come from? What is the purpose of life? What happens to us after we die?

Garry Morgan, professor of intercultural studies at Northwestern College in St. Paul, Minnesota, defines religion as "an organized system of beliefs that answers ultimate questions and commends certain actions or behaviors based on the answers to those questions." Thus, almost all religions have these three basic components: an organized system of beliefs, certain behaviors and actions related to those beliefs, and answers to questions about the unknown. Not all religions have the same belief systems, nor the same behaviors and actions, nor the same answers to ultimate questions. As Garry writes, "Clearly, all religions are not basically the same." But all religions seek to address the fundamental human need to understand the world and our place in it.

First Peter instructs us to "always be ready to make your defense to anyone who demands from you an accounting for the hope that is in you." In other words, as Christians, our religion should make a difference to us in what we believe and how we live. In the *Message* paraphrase, Eugene Peterson put it like this: "Be ready to speak up and tell anyone who asks why you're living the way you are."

Oliver "Buzz" Thomas was the general counsel for the Baptist Joint Committee for Religious Liberty some years ago. After he left the BJC, Buzz became an attorney in private practice and a member of *USA TODAY*'s Board of Contributors. In an opinion piece that appeared in *USA TODAY*, Buzz addressed the question "Why religion?" He offered a variety of answers, including these:

- Worship—"Millions gather each week to acknowledge their higher power."
- The chance to experience community—Buzz says that healthy congregations are "more than civic clubs. They are surrogate families."
- The opportunity to serve others—Especially here in America, we feed the hungry and house the homeless largely through religious organizations.

Yet, as important as worship, community, and service are, Buzz said the greatest contribution of religion is the meaning that it gives to our lives. We all need a sense of purpose and belonging. We all need to find answers to those ultimate questions: Where did we come from? Why are we here? What happens to us after we die? Buzz said those questions are "not amenable to the scientific method."[3] Only religion can answer those ultimate questions: What does it all mean? And how then should we live?

As a pastor, it concerns me that many people, especially younger people, are giving up on religion. I can understand how people might become disillusioned by churches that fail to live out the principles of Jesus. But as flawed and as imperfect as churches can be, what other organization can better provide opportunities for worship and community and service and also give meaning to our lives?

Church historian Bruce Gourley writes that during the latter decades of the 18th century, after the American Revolution, only 7–10 percent of Americans attended church. Gourley explains that after the adoption of the Constitution that provided for the separation of church and state, worship attendance was no longer mandatory, as it had been in many of the colonies. The citizens of the United States had genuine religious freedom, and Gourley says that many of those citizens "exercised their newfound freedom to vacate church pews." In other words, no longer forced to attend worship, no longer subject to involuntary religion, many people stopped going to church because they no longer had to. But this low ebb in church attendance did not last long.

During the Second Great Awakening in the 19th century many Americans discovered authentic religious faith. Freed from the unholy alliance of church and state, many Christian denominations became revitalized and new religious movements began. By the 1830s more than half of all Americans, according to some estimates, were attending religious services. Once people were no longer forced to go to church, voluntary religious expressions were free to thrive. Church attendance thrived for 150 years or more.

Now in the 21st century we are experiencing yet another transition in attitudes toward religious organizations. Younger people are not as involved in institutional Christianity as they once were, to the point where more than one-third of young adults now claim no religious affiliation. Many churches have responded to this challenge by seeking to modernize their styles of worship and by de-emphasizing their denominational identities to broaden their appeal. Some churches have adopted a style of worship, particularly music, that is more rock than classical.

Samuel Lloyd, who served as deacon of Washington National Cathedral, wrote in *The Washington Post*: "Christianity in Europe and North America is going through its biggest period of institutional redefinition in 500 years. An increasingly pluralistic world…saturated with information, choices, and entertainment, seems too busy for church life." Yet Lloyd has not given up on the church. Instead, he said, "the world needs to see concrete examples of generous-spirited, intellectually alive, spiritually profound, interfaith-sensitive, scientifically open, socially engaged Christianity." Lloyd predicts that denominational loyalty will continue to fade. But he has hope that "fresh ways of blending the old with the new will continue to emerge…and that faith will find new forms."[4]

A lot of people outside the church do not even think about God—that is, until a tornado hits, or an illness is diagnosed, or a loved one dies, or some other traumatic event raises those ultimate questions of life. But religion offers so much even when life is not traumatic. Religion offers the opportunity for worship, community, service, and living with a sense of hope day by day. Peter said always be ready to explain the hope that is in you. Be ready to speak up when anyone asks why you are living the way you are. In Jesus Christ we have connections that give meaning to our lives: connections with God, with one another in the family of faith, and with people in need through our calling to service.

In Jesus Christ we have a sense of purpose and a place of belonging. In Jesus Christ we have hope for this world, and hope for the world to come.

Frankly, I feel sorry for people who don't go to church. They don't know what they are missing. But we can tell them. We can show them. We can share the good news. We can explain the hope that is in us. We can speak up about the way we live. Unlike that woman in Oklahoma who didn't thank the Lord because she says she doesn't believe in God, we can thank the Lord every day for his guidance, care, protection, and blessings. In the words of the old hymn, "All good gifts around us are sent from heaven above. Then thank the Lord, oh thank the Lord for all his love."

THE HOPE THAT IS IN YOU, PART 2
(1 Pet. 3:13-18)

The Martin Luther King Jr. Memorial, adjacent to the National Mall in Washington, D.C., was a long time coming. It honors not only the sacrifices of one man who suffered for doing what is right, but also recognizes an era in our national history that we are still trying to make right. The erection of the memorial was a step in the healing journey, as we move beyond the pains of the past toward a future that truly fulfills the American ideals of freedom and justice for all. But the memorial to Dr. King is only a step. There is much more healing that needs to be done.

Jim Wallis, founder of the Christian organization Sojourners, says that racism is America's original sin. Unlike slavery in the Bible, slavery in the American experience was based on racism. One race was presumed to be superior to other races. And that presumption issued not only in slavery, but also in the genocide of Native Americans, in antipathy toward many immigrants, and in a history of racism that has stained our nation to this day. Slavery ended in the 19th century, but the legacy of slavery continues into the 21st century. African Americans have higher rates of poverty, unemployment, incarceration, lack of health insurance, inadequate medical care, and a host of other inequities than any other racial group. The wounds of the past are far from healed.

First Peter 3 is about suffering for doing good, and about healing old wounds. It is about God's prescription for moving beyond the pains of the past, and about finding a way to live together in harmony and peace. If Christ had ruled in the hearts of early European settlers, Native Americans would not have been forced from their lands, and Africans would not have been enslaved. If the early colonists and their descendants had followed Christ's law of love toward their neighbors, they would have treated all people with dignity and respect. But that did not happen. Instead, European colonizers treated Native Americans and Africans as inferior beings. And our society has been wracked by racial divisions ever since. There can be no healing from the wounds of the past without acknowledging the injustices that were committed, and the legacy of those injustices that continue.

Just about everyone knows something about Martin Luther King Jr., but there were many other courageous leaders in the civil rights movement. Many historians consider Fred Shuttlesworth, also a Baptist pastor, to be one of the "Big Three" in the struggle for racial justice. Along with Rev. Ralph Abernathy and Dr. King, Rev. Shuttlesworth founded the Southern Christian Leadership Conference in 1957. Although not as widely recognized as the others, Shuttlesworth was a key figure.

Diane McWhorter, who won the 2002 Pulitzer Prize for her nonfiction chronicle of Birmingham in the 1950s and 1960s, says that Shuttlesworth was as important to the cause as King was. According to McWhorter, "Shuttlesworth and King were the two major axes…of the movement. Shuttlesworth was in the vanguard of direct action, pushing toward confrontation. King was the person who could really deal with white people and was more conciliatory. The two of them formed a dialectic that drove the movement forward."[5]

Fred Shuttlesworth began his social activism while serving as pastor of Bethel Baptist Church in Birmingham in the early 1950s. After the U.S. Supreme Court ruled in 1954 that public school segregation was unconstitutional, Shuttlesworth said, "I felt like I was a man, that I had rights." He became an activist in Birmingham, calling for the hiring of African-American police officers and working to register African Americans to vote. He also supported the bus boycott led by Dr. King in 1955.

When the state of Alabama basically outlawed the NAACP in 1956, Shuttlesworth formed another group to work to end racial segregation. Historian Taylor Branch wrote that this singled Shuttlesworth out as the "preacher courageous enough or crazy enough to defy Bull Connor," the racist public safety commissioner of Birmingham.

On Christmas night of 1956, Rev. Shuttlesworth was inside his parsonage laying plans to lead an effort to integrate the buses in Birmingham, when 15 sticks of dynamite were detonated right outside the house, beneath his bedroom window. The parsonage was destroyed, but Shuttlesworth escaped injury. He emerged from the wreckage shaken but undeterred.

A police officer, who belonged to the Ku Klux Klan, told Shuttlesworth, "If I were you, I'd get out of town as quick as I could." Rev. Shuttlesworth told him to tell the Klan that he was not leaving, saying, "I wasn't saved to run." The next day he led 200 people onto Birmingham's buses. After 21 African-American bus passengers were taken to jail, Shuttlesworth sued the police for wrongful arrest. His congregation built a new parsonage for his family and posted sentries outside to guard against further attacks.

In 1957 Fred Shuttlesworth and his wife Ruby took two of their daughters to enroll in an all-white public school in Birmingham. When they drove up, more than a dozen men were armed with chains, brass knuckles, and baseball bats. The police were nowhere around. The men savagely attacked Shuttlesworth, beating him until he was unconscious. During the attack one of the men stabbed Ruby in the hip. After regaining consciousness, and somehow getting himself and his wife back into the car, he calmly told the driver not to break any traffic laws as they rushed away.

By his own count, Shuttlesworth was bombed twice, beaten into unconsciousness, and jailed more than 35 times. On one occasion during a protest in Birmingham, Bull Connor ordered his officers to shoot fire hoses at the demonstrators. Rev. Shuttlesworth was so seriously injured by the fire-hose blast that he had to be taken to the hospital. Connor told a reporter, "I wish they'd carried him away in a hearse." Rep. John Lewis, who was an eyewitness to many of the events, paid this tribute: "When others did not have the courage to stand up, speak up, and speak out, Fred Shuttlesworth put all he had on the line to end segregation in Birmingham and the state of Alabama."

According his obituary in the *Los Angeles Times*, "Shuttlesworth often said that he 'tried to get killed in Birmingham' to draw attention to the injustices." After the explosion that nearly took his life he said, "God made me bomb-proof."[6] Yet, despite being a victim of violence, Shuttlesworth steadfastly refused to resort to violence himself. The Southern Christian Leadership Conference was founded on the motto: "Not one hair of one head of one person should be harmed."

Fred Shuttlesworth was one of the most courageous leaders in the civil rights movement. As our scripture in 1 Peter said, he suffered for doing what was right, and he refused to be intimidated. He was always ready to give a defense for the hope that was in him. Because of his unshakable faith in God, his commitment to Jesus Christ and his conviction that ultimately truth would prevail, he placed his life on the line again and again for the cause of equality and justice. Years later, when new leaders in Birmingham recognized his heroic actions, they renamed the Birmingham Airport after him. If you fly into Birmingham today, you will land at the Birmingham-Shuttlesworth International Airport.

The genius of the civil rights movement is that it was based on Christian principles of justice, nonviolence, and suffering for righteousness' sake. Reverends King, Abernathy, and Shuttlesworth were just following the example of Jesus, who suffered for righteousness, to bring us to God. Sometimes life is terribly unfair, and people are terribly cruel, and sometimes good people suffer for doing what is right. But God is good, and his mercy endures forever and ultimately justice will prevail. In the meantime, let us do what is right. May we have love for one another, a tender heart, and a humble mind. May we not repay evil for evil or abuse for abuse. May we follow Jesus and give an accounting for the hope that is in us.

THE HOPE THAT IS IN YOU, PART 3
(1 Pet. 3:13-18)

The adventurer Henry Pidgeon traveled around the world by himself in a small sailboat. After his voyage he described the perils of his journey. During one interview, in a bit of role reversal, Pidgeon asked the interviewer a question. "Do you know what is the most dangerous time for a man sailing alone at sea?" The interviewer replied, "Well, I suppose it is during storms, or perhaps sailing near rocks or a coral reef." "No," Pidgeon replied, "the time of greatest danger is when the sea is calm, and a good breeze is blowing." The interviewer did not understand, so Pidgeon explained: "During a storm or among the shoals, the sailor is on the alert. His senses are heightened, his reflexes are on the ready, his mind and body are energized. But in fair weather, he is more relaxed. He is apt to walk around the deck without thinking or holding on. Then a breeze or a roll of the boat can throw him overboard, and he is lost."[7]

I don't know that much about sailing, but Pidgeon's assessment rings true about life. The most dangerous times in life are not necessarily the times of great tumult and personal crisis. The most dangerous times may be when the sea is calm, and everything seems to be going our way. When life is threatening, our senses are aroused, and our faith is on the alert. In times of crisis, we grab hold of anything firm to give us stability; we rediscover the value of religion. In times of crisis, we pray with a sense of urgency and worship with a renewed dedication. But when the crisis passes and things calm down, it is easy to relax our faith a bit. It is easy to become casual about our commitment, to become nonchalant about our spiritual life. When things are going well, we tend to imagine that we have life under control; we forget about God, or at least place God on the back burner of our lives.

In our scripture passage Peter talks about living in a state of perpetual preparation. He advises us to always be prepared, to be on the ready, to be on a "faith alert" so that we can deal with whatever life may bring. Of this we can be sure: Sooner or later, the storms of life will come.

When the Bible talks about sufferings, it really talks about two kinds of sufferings. First, there are the troubles that come to us because we are human. Some amount of suffering is inevitable in every life. For example, most of us sooner or later will experience grief from the death of a friend or a family member. It's unavoidable, a part of being human. Some sufferings come our way simply because we are human. But there is another kind of suffering that comes to us because we are Christians.

Sometimes our Christian faith causes us to suffer. Sometimes, because we are Christians, others treat us in an unjust or unkind way. Peter says that no matter what sufferings come our way, we can overcome them because of the hope that is within us. And the reason we have that hope is because of our faith in Christ. The poet Priscilla Leonard wrote these words:

> No one can choose what coming hours may bring
> To him of need, of joy, of suffering;
> But what his soul shall bring unto each hour
> To meet its challenge—that is in his power.

We cannot choose what life may bring to us, but we can choose what we will bring to life. As Christians, we bring to life a hope that can sustain us no matter what happens. We bring to life a hope grounded in the love of God.

The movie *My Left Foot* tells the story of an Irish man named Christy Brown, who was born in Dublin in 1932 with cerebral palsy, and as a boy was severely disabled. Unable to control his tongue to speak, to control his limbs except for his left foot, and to control his body movements, Christy was a pathetic-looking soul.

At that time, there was no treatment for his condition, so Christy spent his days lying on the floor in a heap underneath the staircase of his modest home. Because he could not communicate, everyone assumed Christy was as mentally deficient as he was physically limited. But one day, when Christy was a teenager, the hospital in Dublin brought in a new doctor who began a program for young victims of cerebral palsy. Christy was older than the other patients and did not fit in at the hospital, so the doctor went to his house and began a rigorous program of physical exercise and speech therapy. The going was slow, but the results were remarkable. Gradually, Christy learned to speak so that he could be understood. Eventually the doctor gave him a copy of the famous soliloquy from *Hamlet* to read aloud and memorize.

In a memorable scene, Christy is upstairs in his bedroom rehearsing the speech. "To be or not to be, that is the question," he says. His speech is slurred, but the words come through. His mother and father are downstairs listening. "I don't like the sound of his voice," his mother says. "What's the matter with his voice?" his father asks. The mother replies, "It's got too much hope in it." Knowing Christy had been disappointed many times before, his mother wanted to protect him from getting hurt again. But it was the hope in his voice that drove Christy to learn to paint with his left foot. It was the hope in his heart that enabled Christy to triumph over the afflictions of his body and to create beautiful works of art.

We Christians have hope in our voices and hope in our hearts. Peter said we should express that hope and share it with others. He said we should always be ready to explain to anyone about the hope that we have within us. We cannot see around the corner into the future, but this we know: God is around every corner in whatever future lies before us. Let the chips fall where they may. We know that the future is in God's hands.

Edgar Jackson was a renowned minister, author, and pastoral counselor. He wrote many books, trained many young pastors, and helped many people with their personal problems. Then Jackson got knocked off his feet by a stroke. For a time, he was partially paralyzed and lost his ability to speak. Gradually, he regained his movement and speech and was able to welcome visitors at his farm in Vermont.

One of his first visitors was a man who had a lot of problems of his own. He admired the way Jackson had overcome his stroke, and he wondered how he could deal with his own difficulties. After they had talked for a while, Jackson took the man out to the pasture behind the house. Years before, a former owner had planted a row of maple trees around the perimeter of the pasture, instead of digging holes and setting posts for a fence. When the maple trees had grown big enough, the former owner had stretched strands of barbed wire from tree to tree to enclose the pasture. Jackson asked his guest to observe how the barbed wire had affected the trees.

Some of the trees were stunted and misshapen, twisted and deformed by the wires that had cut into their trunks. But other trees were tall and strong. Somehow, they had been able to incorporate the wires into their trunks and had grown around them. That, Jackson remarked, is the way it is with people. Some people allow problems and difficulties to so intrude upon their lives that they become twisted and misshapen, or do not grow at all. But others, he said, are like the tall, majestic trees. Somehow, they have learned to incorporate the difficulties of life and to grow straight and strong.[8]

Troubles come to every life. But whether we are stunted and deformed by them or grow straight and tall in spite of them is up to us. The difference is the hope in our hearts. The difference is the living power of Christ the Lord in us.

QUESTIONS FOR DISCUSSION/RELECTION

1. How is it possible not to repay evil for evil?
2. What is the hope that is in you?
3. Have you ever suffered for doing good?
4. How did the suffering of Christ bring us to God?
5. Have you ever tried to explain to someone else the hope that is in you? If so, how?

NOTES

[1] *Time*, June 3, 2013.
[2] *The Washington Post*, June 22, 2013.
[3] *USA Today*, Monday, August 9, 2010.
[4] *The Washington Post*, "On Faith," December 31, 2011.
[5] http://articles.latimes.com/print/2011/oct/06/local/la-me-fred-shuttlesworth-20111006.
[6] *Los Angeles Times*, October 6, 2011
[7] *Preaching*, July-August 1989.
[8] Martin Thielen, *Getting Ready for Sunday's Sermon* (Nashville: BSSB, 1990), 119-120.

CHAPTER 10

LOVE ONE ANOTHER
(1 John 4:7-12)

> *Dear friends, let us love one another, for love comes from God. Everyone who loves has been born of God and knows God. Whoever does not love does not know God, because God is love. This is how God showed his love among us: He sent his one and only Son into the world that we might live through him. This is love: not that we loved God, but that he loved us and sent his Son as an atoning sacrifice for our sins. Dear friends, since God so loved us, we also ought to love one another. No one has ever seen God; but if we love one another, God lives in us and his love is made complete in us.*
>
> (1 John 4:7-12 NIV)

How do we know that God is love? He sent his Son as an atoning sacrifice for our sins. How do we respond to God's love for us? We respond by loving one another. It is our love for one another that shows we have been born of God and know God. Of course, no one has ever seen God. But if we love one another, others will see God in us. They will see that God lives in us and his love is made complete in us. What an awesome calling! We love one another, not through our own strength, but because we live through God's one and only Son that he sent into the world. Love is not something we produce; love comes from God. It is the essential definition of who God is: God is love.

Every Christian has two birthdays: the day we were born, and the day we were born again. Someone has said that the two most important days in your life are the day you were born, and the day you find out why. As Christians, we have found out why were we born. We were born to love God and to love each other. That is the "why" of our birth, and the "why" of our new birth in Christ. As John said, "if we love one another, God lives in us, and his love is made complete in us" (1 John 4:12). To strive to have God's love perfected in us is the "why" of our being. That is the purpose of our lives. And that is the purpose of our life together in the church.

LOVE IN ACTION
(1 John 4:7-8)

Every year my church in Maryland adopted a summer mission project. One summer we worked with City Gate, an urban ministry in Washington, D.C. and Prince George's County, Maryland that seeks to open doors of opportunity to disadvantaged children and youth. Apart from a few members of our Missions Commission, most of our congregants had only a vague idea of what City Gate was about. So, to help our church better understand City Gate, I called its founder and executive director, Lynn Bergfalk. Dr. Bergfalk also served as pastor of Wisconsin Avenue Baptist Church on Tenley Circle in the District. When City Gate was founded in 2000, he was pastor of Calvary Baptist Church near Chinatown in the District. I asked Lynn how it all got started.

Lynn told me that the Calvary congregation was already deeply involved in ministering to their community. The church had a homeless shelter in its building, provided a weekly meal for the homeless, and sponsored an after-school program and summer programs for disadvantaged children and youth in the community. But they wanted to do more. Lynn had a vision of expanding the ministry beyond what Calvary or any one church could do. He had a vision for a non-profit organization that would conduct ministries in various low-income communities. By moving beyond one church, the ministry could be supported by a variety of churches and individuals and foundations.

Lynn was so passionate about beginning this new work that he resigned as pastor of Calvary to devote his complete attention to City Gate. Lynn chose the name, City Gate, because in biblical times, the gate of the city was an important meeting place. The elders of the city would meet there to dispense justice to the poor, the widows, and the orphans. It was a place where strangers in the land would be welcomed. Lynn had a vision that City Gate could fulfill the prophetic vision for justice and mercy in the city of Washington, D.C. and surrounding communities.

Shortly after City Gate was incorporated, the D.C. Baptist Convention was looking for an organization to provide programming for the Johenning Baptist Center in Anacostia. It was a natural fit. The staff of City Gate began to operate out of the Johenning Center, providing after-school and summer programs, meals, and other activities for about 100 children in the community in southeast Washington.

The cooperation between City Gate and the D.C. Baptist Convention continued for several years. But then the Convention had the opportunity to lease the Johenning Baptist Center to a charter school. The income from the charter school would provide for much-needed maintenance to the building. That left City Gate without a base of operations. Yet, what seemed like a crisis became an unforeseen opportunity. Lynn learned about community rooms in low-rent housing complexes only blocks from the Johenning Center. The management company of the housing complexes was looking for an organization to provide programming for children when they were not in school. Again, it was a perfect fit. City Gate began to operate out of these community rooms.

Instead of serving in just one location, City Gate began to minister to children and youth in multiple locations, right where they lived. Thus, City Gate became even more a part of the communities it was seeking to serve. City Gate expanded its outreach even further. Not only are City Gate programs serving children and youth in locations in southeast and northeast Washington, but they are also serving locations in low-income areas of Prince George's County, Maryland.

Dr. Bergfalk took some members of the Village Baptist Missions Commission on a tour of several of those locations. They saw children receiving help with homework, learning to use computers, and enjoying a nutritious meal or snack after school. They saw the care, attention, and love that the City Gate staff members give to the children. Our

Missions Commission members were impressed by what they saw, so much so that they recommended our church make City Gate our summer mission project.

You might wonder what City Gate has to do with 1 John 4. Well, City Gate is that scripture passage in action. It is about love. Love is not just something we feel; love is something we do. John wrote, "Beloved, let us love one another." It was like an echo of what Jesus said, that the two greatest commandments are to love God and to love our neighbors as we love ourselves. Again, Jesus was talking about love as more than a feeling. Love is an action.

Here is another story of love in action. Hannah Hawkins was a long-time friend of our church. We got to know Hannah through another mission partner, Here's Life Inner City. Back in 1970, Hannah suffered a great tragedy when her husband was murdered. She was left as a young widow with five children to raise by herself. Hannah said she felt devastated, with no support system. In her anguish, Hannah made a covenant with God. She vowed that if God would give her the strength to get out of bed every day and do what she needed to do to take care of her children, then she would serve those who are less fortunate. Eventually, her pledge became a full-time job.

It started out in her own home in the early 1980s when she founded a ministry to neighborhood children. She began providing hot meals every day for children in the neighborhood who otherwise would have gone hungry. She also found a way to provide clothing and tutoring for children between the ages of 4 and 18. At first, she used her own money. Later, Mrs. Hawkins moved the program, which she called, "Children of Mine," to two abandoned apartments in a housing project in southeast Washington, D.C. called Sheridan Terrace. It was a time when that area of Anacostia was infested with drug dealers and gangs. There were drive-by shootings and murders almost every week.

In 1992 the Children of Mine Youth Center relocated to a house in southeast D.C. that had been abandoned and neglected for years. Mrs. Hawkins contacted the owners of the property and asked them if she could rent the building to continue providing services to children in the community, services similar to those provided by City Gate. Many of the children came from homes where there was chronic substance abuse. Often they would have to fend for themselves after school and during the summer months. Mrs. Hawkins had a vision to help these young people from becoming children in crisis to becoming children who realized their God-given potential. Mrs. Hawkins said, children "are just like sponges. They will absorb anything that you give them. I will say to you just like I say to them every night, 'Poison in, poison out. Love in, love out.' And that's what we try to give them: love, consistency, understanding, and patience."

Sulaiman Harris was 6 years old when he started coming to Children of Mine in 1988. Harris said Mrs. Hawkins offered a "safe haven" from the streets, with meals, tutoring, arts and crafts, and other activities. Harris said, "It was the first place that many of us learned manners, 'yes sir, yes ma'am, thank you.'" With Mrs. Hawkins' encouragement, Harris received full scholarships to Archbishop Carroll High School and then to the University of Pittsburg, where he earned a degree in electrical engineering. Later he received a master's degree from Strayer University in information systems. Harris found a job as a contract project manager with the General Services Administration of the federal government. On weekends, Harris would come back regularly to Children of Mine. He helped feed the homeless. He gave haircuts to men getting ready to go out on job interviews. Sulaiman Harris also understands love in action.

Village Baptist Church provided Christmas shoeboxes for the children and youth of Children of Mine. Some years Hannah would give us a list of more than 100 names. Like the staff and volunteers at City Gate, the staff and volunteers at Children of Mine put their love into action. My church was involved with Children of Mine for many years, and we began supporting City Gate through the Souper Bowl of Caring offering on Super Bowl Sundays. Then we stepped up our support for City Gate through our summer mission project.

Visionaries such as Lynn Bergfalk and Hannah Hawkins showed us that love is not just something you feel. Love is something you do. We put our love into action because God first loved us. God put his love into action when he sent us his Son. "Beloved, let us love one another; because love is from God; everyone who loves is born of God and knows God. Whoever does not love does not know God, for God is love."

WHO CARES?
(1 John 4:7-21)

Mental health counselor Rose Schrott, who had an office in the Village Baptist Church building, invited me to go with her to a suicide prevention seminar at the Bowie City Hall. At first, I was reluctant to go. The seminar was on Thursday, my day off. Plus, the subject matter was not exactly enticing. Still, I went and I was grateful I did. I learned some things about suicide, and about how to recognize the danger signs and try to prevent it. For example, I was reminded that everyone at some time is affected by anxiety, or depression, or fear, or anger, or frustration, or stress. None of us is immune to those pressures that can push a person over the edge. The seminar reminded me that the only way to prevent suicides is personal involvement. It is a matter of being aware of the warning signs and caring enough to intervene or get help. Although I'm not specifically focusing on suicide prevention here, let me briefly highlight some things to be aware of in the behavior of a family member, or a neighbor, or a co-worker, or a friend:

- changes in actions or behaviors
- a change in eating habits or sleeping patterns
- excessive use of drugs or alcohol
- a rapid drop in grades at school
- the sudden lack of interest in work
- an impulsive desire to give away personal possessions
- personality changes such as emotional outbursts or mood swings
- long-lasting depression
- the death of a family member or friend
- a relationship break-up
- the loss of a job
- a major disappointment or failure

These signs do not always mean that a person is thinking about suicide, but they are reasons to pay attention.

Now, what does all of this have to do with 1 John 4? More than you might imagine. This is one of the most important chapters in the Bible because it tells who God is and what we are supposed to do. It is rather comprehensive and contains the most famous statement in all scripture, "God is love." It tells us what we are to do as Christians, namely, "love one another." You might even call it "the love chapter," except that title has already been given to Paul's 1 Corinthians 13. But I went back and counted. The word "love" occurs 10 times in 1 Corinthians, but in 1 John 4, "love" is used as a noun or a verb 25 times. Clearly, love is at the center of 1 John 4, and it is at the center of our faith.

Unfortunately, love has become such an overused word that we may have forgotten what it really means. The Greeks had at least three distinct words for love: *eros*, *philia*, and *agape*. But we use the one word "love" to refer to a whole range of attitudes and emotions. Perhaps most common is the way we use "love" to mean "like." We love that which we like or enjoy or that which gives us pleasure. I love ice cream. I love playing golf. I love listening to music. You get the idea.

In 1 John and throughout the New Testament, love has a different meaning. *Agape* (love) is the theme; it is far deeper than that which we like or enjoy. *Agape* was a special word. It was rarely used outside the New Testament in secular literature. We know of only a few occasions when secular Greek writers used the word *agape* at all. Apparently, it was the early Christian writers—for example, Paul and John—who took this obscure Greek word, *agape*, and gave it a new depth of meaning. *Agape* is God's kind of love. *Agape* is love that comes from God and that is the supreme characteristic of the Christian life. *Agape* is the kind of unselfish, unmerited, unconditional love that God has for us, and that God wants us to have for one another. And yes, *agape* can be a difficult and costly kind of love. It is the kind of love that gets us personally involved.

Maybe instead of using the word "love," we should use the word "care." Read 1 John 4:7-12, substituting the word "care" for the word "love" in each instance. That is what it is all about—caring. God cares for us, and God wants us to care for one another. According to 1 John, there is nothing more important we can do. It is the bottom line to our religion: Do we care?

The call came around midnight. It was a nurse at the hospital asking me to come at once. The family had asked for me to come. They were not members of our church. I only knew the son, who had attended some youth group meetings at our church years before. But I could tell from the nurse's voice that something was terribly wrong. She would not elaborate, only that I was to come to the hospital right away. I threw on some clothes and headed out, not sure what to expect. It was the worst. The mother of this family, a mental patient at the hospital, had committed suicide. She had hanged herself in her hospital room. The family was distraught beyond description. The hospital staff was obviously upset that such a thing could happen on their watch. And here I was, called out in the middle of the night to meet with a family I hardly knew, called as a man of God to do something. What could I possibly do in a situation like that, but love?

Agape love does not necessarily involve something we like. I did not like being called out in the middle of the night. I did not like driving in the dark, literally and figuratively, to the hospital. I did not like sitting on the floor of that hospital room with the lifeless body of the mother lying on the bed only a few feet away. I did not like trying to console her husband as he sat on the floor beside, me sobbing uncontrollably into his hands. I did not like having to deal with the guilt of the shaken psychiatrist and the nurses who had let this happen. No, I did not like any of it. It was tough, it was hard, and it was gut-wrenching, but I did not regret going.

I had no regrets because, as a Christian, I had to be there. As a Christian, I was called to step right into the middle of that terrible mess, and to do what I could. I was called to be there because God does not expect us to go any place he has not already gone. We love because God first loved us. We love because God has been loving us all along. We love because God has stepped right into the middle of the terrible mess that our lives sometimes become, and God has done something. We have no higher calling on this earth than to care. And sometimes caring costs; sometimes caring hurts. But in the end, it just may be the only thing that really matters.

God calls us to love one another. And that means to love the very real people in the very real places where we live. Sometimes this is hard to do. Sometimes it is hard to love that co-worker, that neighbor across the street, that fellow church member, that family member. But in the end, it is our love for other people, our care for other people, that is the litmus test of our faith. John said the way to show that we love God, whom we cannot see, is to love those persons around us whom we can see.

Back in the fourth century the Christian scholar Jerome told a story about John, the author of our scripture text. Jerome said that when John grew so old and so weak that he could no longer preach, he would be carried into the assembly and be set before the congregation. Then, in a voice barely above a whisper, John would say, over and over again, "Little children, love one another; little children, love one another." Of course, John was admired and respected, but after a while, the people grew tired of hearing him say the same thing time and again. Finally, they asked him why he could say nothing else. Without hesitating, John replied: "I say it because it is the Lord's command, and if only this be done, it is enough."

Perhaps you will never have to deal with a person contemplating suicide. Perhaps you will never have to console a family after it has happened. But whether you realize it or not, you may already be there. Likely, there are people around you who are killing themselves, in one way or another. Probably there are people in your network of relationships who are dying for want of love. But you can do something about it. No matter who you are, no matter how much you know, no matter what gifts you have or do not have, you can do something about it. You can care. "Little children," John said, "love one another." Somehow, it is enough.

THREE LEVELS OF LOVE
(Phil. 2:3-11)

The Bible speaks of different levels of love. In the Greek language there are several different words for love. C.S. Lewis, in his book, *The Four Loves*, identifies four of those words.

- *Storge* denotes affection. A form of the word appears once in the New Testament, in Romans 12:10, where Paul wrote, "Love one another with mutual affection."
- *Philia* is friendship love, or brotherly love. The city of Philadelphia was named after this kind of love. *Philia* (or the verb form *phileo*) appears a couple of dozen times in the New Testament.
- *Eros* refers to romantic love. Although popular in secular Greek literature, this word does not occur in the New Testament. It's not that the Bible has anything against romantic love—read the Song of Songs.
- *Agape* means unconditional love, God's kind of love. The dominant New Testament term for love, the noun *agape* and the verb *agapao* occur some 250 times in the New Testament.

Interestingly, *agape* and *agapao* do not occur frequently in secular Greek literature. The other Greek words for love were far more common. But the Greek translation of the Old Testament used *agapao* to translate the Hebrew verb for love. And the New Testament writers adopted *agapao* as the dominant verb for love, in preference to the more common Greek words. In fact, the word *agape* seems to have been invented by the New Testament writers as a term for God's love, derived from the verb *agapao*.

Based on the title of this section, "Three Levels of Love," you might guess that I would be noting the differences between those Greek words for love, except that I mentioned four words, and not three. Three of the four Greek words for love do occur in the New Testament, but this section is all about *agape*, God's unconditional love for us, and the unconditional love that God wants us to have for each other. I would suggest there are three levels of *agape*, based on specific teachings about love from Jesus.

"Enemy love" is based on Jesus' command in Matthew 5:43-46 to "love your enemies." You might think that loving your enemies is the highest level of *agape*, but I am suggesting that it is really the basic level of love. "Enemy Love" is *Agape* 101, the starting level of unconditional love. Jesus said, "love your enemies, and pray for those who persecute you" (Matt. 5:44). Instead of seeking revenge against our enemies, we are to pray for them, and yes, to love them. If that is the basic level of love, you can see we have some climbing to do!

"Neighbor love" is a higher level of love, higher even than loving our enemies. In Matthew 22:39 Jesus commands, "Love your neighbor as yourself." Jesus said this is the second greatest commandment, second only to loving God. We are to love our neighbors as ourselves. What makes this a higher level of love is the modifier, "as you love yourself." I certainly don't love my enemies as I love myself. But "neighbor love" is greater than enemy love. Love for my neighbor is raised to the level of love for myself. Now, there is something right about healthy self-love. A person who does not love herself or himself is a troubled person. Healthy self-love is a good thing: it means that we take care of ourselves, make wise choices, and value the gifts of life and health and well-being that God has given us. There is something good about healthy self-love. The problem is when self-love becomes idolatrous, when we love ourselves above all else, including above God.

In commanding this second level of love, Jesus said that we are to raise our regard for the well-being of our neighbor to the level of our regard for the well-being of ourselves. If I love my neighbor as I love myself, I want the best for that other person. I set that other person's well-being right alongside my own. An example of "neighbor love" is the marriage relationship. In marriage, my partner's needs are just as important as my needs. The only way that can work, with an unconditional commitment to the other person, is if both marriage partners promise to do it. They take care of one another's needs without worrying about whether their own needs will be met. This is "neighbor love," a higher level of *agape*.

"Christ love" is the ultimate level of love. In John 13 Jesus said, "I give you a new commandment, that you love one another." At first hearing, this does not sound like a new commandment, but rather an extension of the commandments Jesus had given before: love your enemies, love your neighbors. But here is what makes the commandment new: Jesus said, "just as I have loved you, you also should love one another." The first level of *agape* is enemy love—to love our enemies and pray for those who persecute us. The second level of *agape* is neighbor love—to love our neighbors as we love ourselves. The third level of *agape*, the highest level, is Christ love—to love one another as Jesus loves us. This is the highest level because Jesus loves us even more than we love ourselves. Jesus loved us so much that he laid down his life for us. Jesus loved us with God's love, *agape* in its purest form. There is no greater love than that.

Thomas Dorsey was born in rural Georgia in 1899, the son of an itinerant preacher. He dropped out of school at the age of 12 to make a living playing the piano at house parties in African-American communities around Atlanta. In his early 20s, he moved to Chicago, playing blues music and writing his own compositions in honky-tonks and other venues.

In 1925 Dorsey married Nettie Harper, but soon after their marriage he experienced a nervous breakdown and was unable to work for two years. Nettie supported the two of them by working in a laundry. At the urging of his sister-in-law, Thomas attended a church service where he had a spiritual revival. That experience, along with the untimely death of a young neighbor, led Thomas to recommit his life to Christ and to use his music for Christian service. As an expression of this new focus in life, Dorsey wrote his first gospel song.

In 1932 Thomas Dorsey became the choir director of the Pilgrim Baptist Church in Chicago. The country was in the midst of the Great Depression, and Dorsey saw his music as a way to lift people's spirits and give them hope. In August of that year he was the featured soloist at a large revival meeting in St. Louis. Nettie was pregnant with their first child, and she remained in their tiny apartment on the south side of Chicago while Thomas traveled to St. Louis.

On the first night of the revival meeting, after he had finished playing, Thomas was handed a Western Union telegram. He ripped open the envelope, and pasted on the yellow sheet were the words, "Your wife just died." Thomas hurried back to Chicago where he learned that his wife had died in childbirth, having given her life in giving life to a baby boy. Yet, that night the baby died too. Thomas buried his beloved Nettie and their newborn son together in the same casket. He got through the visitation and the funeral, but after it was all over, he withdrew into a deep depression. Thomas later recalled, "I felt that God had done me an injustice. I didn't want to serve him anymore or write gospel songs. I just wanted to go back to the jazz world I knew so well."

A friend visited Thomas in his despair. The friend didn't know what to say, but he was there to show he cared. After consoling Thomas as he could, the friend left him alone in a room with a piano. For the first time in many days, Thomas sat at the piano and began to tap the keys. As he haltingly played note after note, he began to feel a sense of peace. He said, "I felt as though I could reach out and touch God." He found himself playing a melody, and the words of a new song came into his head.

Out of that experience was born the gospel song, "Precious Lord, Take My Hand." Eventually the song became known worldwide. It was recorded by Mahalia Jackson and by Elvis Presley in the 1950s. Since then it has been recorded by Aretha Franklin, Merle Haggard, Randy Travis, Faith Hill, and many others. It was Martin Luther King Jr.'s favorite gospel song and was sung at Dr. King's funeral. It was also sung at the funeral of President Lyndon Johnson.

Thomas Dorsey died in 1993, having served for more than 40 years as choir director of Pilgrim Baptist Church in Chicago. *The Washington Post* obituary called Thomas Dorsey the "Father of Gospel Music," for his merging of religious music with blues and ragtime. His message of the love of God lives on.[1]

John said it in 1 John 4: "Dear friends, let us love one another, for love comes from God. Everyone who loves has been born of God and knows God. Dear friends, since God so loved us, we also ought to love one another."

QUESTIONS FOR DISCUSSION/REFLECTION

1. What does it mean to "love one another"?
2. How do we know that "God is love"?
3. What is the difference between human love and God's love?
4. What is the connection between our love for God and our love for other people?
5. How can God's love be made complete in us?

NOTE

[1] Based on "The Story Behind the Song," by Victor Parachin, ChristianityToday.com.

About the Author

Bruce Salmon served for 33 years as pastor of Village Baptist Church in Bowie, Maryland. During that time, he preached almost 1,500 original Sunday morning sermons, including 108 sermons based on passages from Acts, 24 from Hebrews, 26 from James, 32 from 1 Peter, and 15 from 1 John. For the last 18 years of his ministry, he taught a Sunday morning pastor's class in which adults read and discussed entire books of the Bible. He also led winter, summer, and Lenten Sunday evening adult studies that covered various topics and Bible books, including the following:

- Introducing the New Testament
- The Sermon on the Mount
- The Life of Christ
- The Life of Paul
- The Passion of Jesus
- The Jesus of the Bible
- Genesis
- Exodus
- Joshua
- 1 Samuel
- 2 Samuel
- Isaiah
- Ezekiel
- Malachi
- Matthew
- Mark
- Luke
- John
- Acts
- Romans
- 2 Corinthians
- Hebrews
- James
- Revelation

A native of Fort Worth, Texas, Salmon received the Bachelor of Arts with a major in English from Baylor University and the Master of Divinity and Doctor of Ministry degrees from the Southern Baptist Theological Seminary. He also received the Master of Arts in Counseling Psychology from Bowie State University, with a specialization in Clinical Pastoral Counseling.

Salmon has served on several committees of the D.C. Baptist Convention and on several commissions of the Baptist World Alliance. In addition to this volume and others in the series *Spelunking Scripture*,* he is the author of *Storytelling in Preaching* (BSSB, 1988) and *Preaching for the Long Haul: A Case Study on Long-term Pastoral Ministry* (Nurturing Faith, 2019).

Salmon is husband to wife Linda, father to grown children Amy and Marc, father-in-law to Stacey, and grandfather to granddaughter Ford. In addition to studying the Bible, his interests include spectator sports, current events, music, museums, golf, and travel.

*For more information and blogs, visit www.spelunkingscripture.com.

www.ingramcontent.com/pod-product-compliance
Lightning Source LLC
Chambersburg PA
CBHW071009160426
43193CB00012B/1983